The
CULTURE
of THEOLOGY

The
CULTURE
of THEOLOGY

John Webster

Edited by
Ivor J. Davidson
and Alden C. McCray

Baker Academic
a division of Baker Publishing Group
Grand Rapids, Michigan

© 2019 by Baker Publishing Group

Published by Baker Academic
a division of Baker Publishing Group
PO Box 6287, Grand Rapids, MI 49516-6287
www.bakeracademic.com

Printed in the United States of America

Library of Congress Cataloging-in-Publication Data
Names: Webster, John, 1955–2016, author. | Davidson, Ivor J., editor.
Title: The culture of theology / John Webster ; edited by Ivor J. Davidson and Alden C. McCray.
Description: Grand Rapids : Baker Academic, a division of Baker Publishing Group, 2019. | Includes bibliographical references and index.
Identifiers: LCCN 2019003751 | ISBN 9781540960801 (cloth)
Subjects: LCSH: Theology.
Classification: LCC BR118 .W395 2019 | DDC 230.01—dc23
LC record available at https://lccn.loc.gov/2019003751

19   20   21   22   23   24   25   7   6   5   4   3   2   1

Contents

Acknowledgments

IN MOST BOOKS, authors thank those who have helped them; in this one, the others must chiefly thank the author. The editors gladly register their enduring debts to John Webster for the stimulus of his work; it has been a privilege as ever to spend time with his writing and learn from it afresh. They are grateful also to all who have facilitated their own little bit of labor: to the editors of *Stimulus* for gracious permission to present the text in this new form, and to Fiona Sherwin in particular for her considerable help; to Dave Nelson at Baker Publishing Group for his great enthusiasm for the project and his skill and generosity in steering it toward publication; to Melisa Blok and her colleagues for their dedicated work in the press.

Others have provided encouragement in the venture or been instruments of its possibility. Ivor Davidson is glad in particular to express gratitude to his former colleague at the University of Otago, Professor Paul Trebilco, for his vital role in the organization of the Burns Lectures back in 1998, and trusts that rereading them will rekindle memories of the very happy time we shared with John and his family in Dunedin on that occasion. Hosting these lectures together with Paul and other colleagues at Otago and elsewhere in New Zealand was a joy; extensive further discussion of the material with students over the years since has enhanced appreciation of its depths and invariably reminded of the riches they contain. May this edition extend their appeal and stimulate other fruitful conversations. Above all, may readers appropriate and apply whatever is true and wise in the vision of theology here presented, to the glory of the God of the gospel.

Alden McCray is grateful to Louise for her abiding encouragement: she has especially supported him in this project, sharing his deep gratitude for John. Ivor Davidson accomplishes nothing ever, nor could imagine doing so, but for Julie and Catriona.

Introduction

IVOR J. DAVIDSON

WHAT FOLLOWS IN THIS LITTLE VOLUME is a brief account of the nature and tasks of Christian theology. The theme absorbed its author for life; this particular expression of his thought has been a somewhat neglected jewel in his literary legacy.

John Webster was a theologian's theologian.[1] If anyone in the recent history of the discipline has pondered what it means to do Christian theology "theologically"—as distinct from some other way—he did. What we have here is one statement of that vision, and a few of its practical entailments. The accents belong in a particular phase of their author's development and do not say everything as he would later have said it. For Webster, an Oxford chair counted as mid-career achievement;[2] *The Culture of Theology* was produced within his second year in that position. In later years he felt aspects

---

1. For a brief overview of his career, see Ivor J. Davidson, "John," in *Theological Theology: Essays in Honour of John Webster*, ed. R. David Nelson, Darren Sarisky, and Justin Stratis (New York: Bloomsbury T&T Clark, 2015), 17–36; also Ivor J. Davidson, "In Memoriam: John Webster (1955–2016)," *International Journal of Systematic Theology* 18 (2016): 360–75.

2. Webster was Lady Margaret Professor of Divinity at the University of Oxford from 1996 until 2003. He had previously held positions at St. John's College, Durham (1982–86), and Wycliffe College, Toronto (1986–96). He left Oxford to be Professor of

of his work in this period lacked nuance or required qualification; the underlying instincts could be expressed better, and with less risk of distortion, by bringing a number of other emphases to the fore, locating the practices of theology on a still more specific and yet grander scale. Some differences would emerge. But the argument in this text expounds a number of principles to which he remained strongly committed and presents a fundamental view of its subject from which he did not greatly depart; it gives indication of how those convictions had taken form at that stage in his career and of some of his key concerns at the time.

Though the scale of the work is relatively modest, it remains one of the fullest and most integrated examples of Webster's thinking on how the practice of theology ought to be approached. He went on to write other studies that expand on several of the themes and qualify some of the investments. Those studies were envisaged as preliminary to a multivolume exposition of systematic theology in which he would set out his sense of the discipline at large, the culmination of a further two decades of reflection. His sudden death on May 25, 2016, deprived us of that: the completion of even the first part of the project was not to be. Webster thought of *The Culture of Theology* as a staging post; as things are, it stands as one of his more substantial endeavors to reflect holistically on the privileges, resources, and responsibilities of theological work. He considered the text inchoate: self-conscious, over-invested in the language of cultural practices, not yet clear enough on a doctrine of creation or history or on the abundance of God's Godness as basis of God's outer works, and thus as beginning and end of everything the theologian ever is or does. This had been an early and fairly brief venture on a vast matter; refinements were in order, and a number were adumbrated. Yet this little work sets much before us in a style that remained its author's own; in its elegance, coherence, and conceptual power it offers a magisterial short treatment of what Christian theology is all about, and what it means to take it seriously.

Webster wrote and presented the material as a series of six lectures, the Thomas Burns Memorial Lectures at the University of Otago, Dunedin, New Zealand, in mid-August 1998. The series contributed

---

Systematic Theology at the University of Aberdeen (2003–13). His last appointment was as Professor of Divinity at the University of St. Andrews (2013–16).

to a distinguished academic tradition, endowed in the name of the first chancellor of New Zealand's oldest university. The lectures were delivered over a two-week period[3] and were open to a general audience—theologians and biblical scholars, academics from other disciplines, church leaders, and members of the public. They were published shortly afterward in the New Zealand journal *Stimulus* but have not been reprinted elsewhere.[4] Their instruction has been relished by those in the know; it is high time for the beneficiaries to increase.

I

Webster's overarching argument is quite simple. Christian theology's principal setting is not, he proposes in his opening lecture, its intellectual or social context but "the world which is brought into being by the staggering good news of Jesus Christ" (43). Christian thought and speech about God and about all things else in relation to God are features of Christian *culture*: they take place, first and foremost, in an *eschatological* space, the sphere in which Christian faith and life have their existence by the miracle of God's grace. Christian theology

3. Lectures 1–3 in the first week, 4–6 in the second. Versions of the lectures were also delivered elsewhere in New Zealand; financial support for Webster's visit was contributed by the University of Otago, the Presbyterian Church Synod of Otago and Southland, the Anglican Church, and Bible Society New Zealand.

4. *Stimulus* 6, no. 4 (November 1998): 2–23 (lectures 1–3); *Stimulus* 7, no. 1 (February 1999): 2–20 (lectures 4–6). The published versions replicate the manuscript prepared for the lectures, including its idiom. The text that follows in this volume reproduces this with permission, though minor typographical and stylistic corrections have been made, and the present version adopts US style. Webster's quotations and references have been standardized and at numerous points corrected. The textual divisions in the lectures are Webster's. The present editors have also had access to a copy of Webster's original typescript for the lectures, which has at one point supplied a section of text missing (with loss to the sense) in the *Stimulus* version: see lecture 6 (138–40). A roughly edited version of the typescript for lecture 2 forms the bulk of the essay published as John Webster, "Scripture, Reading, and the Rhetoric of Theology in Hans Frei's Analysis of Texts," in *Ten Year Commemoration to the Life of Hans Frei (1922–1988)*, ed. Giorgy Olegovich (New York: Semenenko Foundation, 1999), 41–53; it may clarify the representation of one paragraph in lecture 2 (72). All substantive editorial emendations or additional comments in the present volume appear in square brackets in the footnotes.

flourishes when its roots in that territory are deep; it withers when
its tasks are pursued in detachment from the traditions of belief and
practice in which alone its work can prosper. In late modernity, the
practice of theology has been inhibited not so much by outward
circumstances—the challenges posed by an intellectual, social, or
political environment—as by internal disorder. All too often, theology
has become dislocated from its most fundamental context; it has
lost sight of the resources, responsibilities, and prospects that situation affords. Remedy lies in the "reintegration" of Christian theology
into the true culture of Christian faith—the church, its texts and
traditions—and in the deployment of genuinely theological categories
in the conception and practice of theological work. Whatever their
historical setting may be, theology's practitioners need to cultivate
habits of mind and soul befitting those for whom the gospel itself is
the most important reality.

The first lecture begins with a basic thesis: "Christian theology
is an activity in a culture which reaches out toward [the] miracle"
that is the "comprehensive interruption of all things in Jesus Christ"
(43). Webster then proceeds to define more closely what he means
by "culture." The term refers to theology's activity as occurring in
a social space, characterized by its own practices, forms, modes of
engagement with other worlds, and strategies for submitting itself to
judgment: theology is undertaken in "the strange world of the gospel
and the church" (44). Existing within a culture, theology needs to be
cultivated, not least through habits of reading, both in Scripture and
in classical Christian texts. Theology accordingly involves *formation*:
the cultivation of persons shaped by the culture of Christian faith.
"Good theological practice depends on good theologians" (45).

Webster is aware that the language of "culture" has limitations.
Christian faith is not simply a human project; as eschatological, it
is never domesticable: "The culture of Christian faith and therefore
the culture of theology stand beneath the sign of their contradiction, which is the gospel of God" (46). Christian faith and theology
are also an *anti*-culture, "the site of a struggle against . . . domestic
idolatry" (47), and the cultivation of Christian culture includes—
vitally—self-critique and repentance. The intellectual activities of
theology are not detached mental acts or transcendent forms of judg-

ment but practices within a particular kind of region; the culture of faith is unlike any other, for it is reliant for its existence, continuity, and final consummation upon the gratuitous purposes and action of God. Theology's culture originates in a divine summons and is directed toward the manifestation of God's glory; on the way to that *telos*, its place is one in which human life is caught up into the process of *conversion*, the pattern of being overthrown and re-established by divine grace. Theology is thus "poised uneasily between location and dislocation" (55). On the one hand, it is fixed, a positive rather than a free science, summoned into being, sustained, and directed by the specific movement declared in the gospel of Jesus Christ; on the other, it is fixed upon the living God, the judge, whose presence and action remain overwhelming, untamable, disturbing. God is no passive object or item of cultural capital; God is living subject, his presence to us sovereign, eloquent, intrusive, dangerous. Theology's practice accordingly calls for both *roots* and *astonishment*: theologians must learn what it means to belong within a territory, with all its vast privileges and resources; but they must also express amazement, inasmuch as all of their living and thinking takes place "in the presence of Easter" (61).

The second lecture sets about the task of defining more closely the place of texts in theological work, in particular the place of Holy Scripture as "the primary bearer of Christian culture" (65). Noting that a good deal of modern church life demonstrates a loss of confidence in Scripture, Webster suggests that the roots of the problem lie not so much in the perceived consequences of historical-critical methods as in "a failure of socialization" (66);[5] the answer is to be found not merely in better theoretical arguments about the nature of the Bible or the mode of its production but by learning what it means to "inhabit" Scripture, to "think and speak as people of the gospel" (66). Pursuit of this goal means frank eschewal of general hermeneutics and the articulation to the contrary of a *theological* account of Scripture and its reading. But a theological account itself must be located in the right doctrinal place: not as a treatment *a priori* of whether or how God might be said to speak, but as an

5. The phrase is taken from Kathryn Tanner, *God and Creation in Christian Theology: Tyranny or Empowerment?* (Oxford: Blackwell, 1988), 169.

a posteriori depiction of the identity of God who speaks and of those whom God addresses. Holy Scripture is the instrument of divine self-communication, the means by which "the mortifying and vivifying self-manifestation of God addresses the church, slaying and making alive" (71). The intrusive force of Scripture's power is to be emphasized; the authority of the Word is interruptive and critical, never a matter for the church's control, a reality to be acknowledged rather than ascribed.

Local hermeneutical culture in evangelical context involves the elaboration not so much of a set of interpretative tactics as an anthropology of the reader. The Christian reader of the Bible is situated in the history of divine salvation; "Christian acts of reading Holy Scripture are encounters between the gracious, eloquent God of the gospel and the sinner who has been arrested and made new" (74). What is required is "teachableness" (74; cf. 146), humble submission to the transformative dynamic of being overthrown and remade by the divine address. Theological discourse stands in necessary relation to this disposition; if theology's language seeks to persuade, to engage its readers so as to shape their beliefs and influence their behavior, it must do so in particular terms. The kind of rhetoric fitting to theology's culture is, first, the rhetoric of effacement, an attentive, ascetic reading of Scripture, a hearing of the Word that has already been spoken. "It is . . . of prime importance to avoid construing theology as a set of improvements upon Scripture" (77). Repetition of Scripture, a modest, transparent articulation of the Word, not some attempt to displace it with human cleverness, is vital. But, second, a rhetoric of edification is called for: theology depicts so as to commend the gospel, to form disciples in spiritual and moral terms. In light of these convictions, which he sees as deeply embedded in classical approaches to the relationship between exegesis, doctrine, and ethics, Webster commends the primacy of meditation upon the biblical text; perhaps "theologians should consider ceasing to write systematic treatises and confine themselves to the work of exposition of Scripture" (80).

If the second lecture is concerned with texts, the third considers traditions, the socially embodied forms in which Christian confession exists in the particular history that applies to the church. The language of a "public covenant" for faith is taken from Kant, but the burden of Webster's argument is to push in precisely the opposite direction from Kant's contrast between a pure religion of interiority and the outward forms found in historical or ecclesiastical faith. Once again, specificity is essential: Christian theology requires an account of tradition that is "decisively shaped by theological factors," not a general case about the constitutive role of Christian traditions in human life and thought but a tracing of the particular sort of culture in which faith is set—"the permanent revolution to which the gospel gives rise" (84). To talk of tradition here is to speak of the apostolicity of the church, and that is less a reference *backward* than *upward*, to the presence of the risen Jesus to the church in the power of the Holy Spirit. Care is needed to phrase the matter aright if the material content of Christian confession is not to dissolve into an account of churchly practices, or if the dangers of ecclesial inflation are avoided only by recourse to a minimalist or apophatic doctrine of God. Theology's understanding of tradition must posit the operative, communicative presence of the risen and ascended Christ and the work of the Spirit.

Webster presents an account of the presence of Christ in the Spirit's power that emphasizes the uniqueness of the exalted Christ as agent of his own presence and avoids equation of the church's role with his. The gratuitousness with which the church is declared to be the body of Christ is important; "however much it may live 'in Christ,' the public covenant of the church is no second Christ, no extension or prolongation of his presence" (91). Tradition is certainly a historical, visible reality, but the visibility of the church is also special, a "spiritual event of assembly around, and life from, the summons of God in Christ through the Spirit" (92). The community constituted by divine action is apostolic, appointed, called, commissioned, and generated by the free Lord. Its task is witness: the confession and proclamation of his prior reality and the freedom in which he ever comes to us, the one who is "indefatigably alive" (96). Theology is one of the ways in which the Christian tradition inquires into its apostolic character. The task is descriptive or didactic, the orderly depiction of the Christian good news; it is also critical, a form of protest against the church's tendency to naturalize or routinize the gospel's revolution. Attentiveness to the gospel means, once more, submission to Scripture, the instrument by which de-eschatologizing of tradition is prevented. Theology's work involves indicating the reality of the living Jesus and also countering the drift of tradition into stasis or self-satisfaction.

Having mapped the culture of Christian faith in a strongly eschatological projection in lectures 1–3, Webster turns in the second half of the series to address an obvious concern: Can theology so conceived actually be done in practice? Lectures 4–6 aspire to offer, respectively, "a politics, a critical theory, and an ethics of the theological task" (100). Lecture 4 considers in particular the place of Christian theology in the modern research university. Webster suggests that the subject is often approached in the wrong way. Instead of asking "What sort of discipline does Christian theology need to be if it is to be accorded a place in the public academy?" we might be better to ask this: "What sort of institution might the academy have to become if it is to profit from having Christian theology as a contributor to its conversations?" (102). What is needed is a better politics of intellectual exchange, or (to borrow a further term from Kant) a better "conflict of the faculties," understood as a meaningful conversation in which there is argument that recognizes genuine *difference*. Theology's contribution to the university is not made by "suspending its strong concerns," far less by the "deadly role" of purveying so-called values, but by "*nonconformity*: an unanxious pursuit of its own proper concerns" (103). Theology must be *itself*.

As Webster explains in lecture 4, contest of the faculties means abandonment of naive ideas of all disciplines as subject to the tribunal of reason, somehow detached from the constitutive role of traditions; it equally requires refusal of a postmodern idealizing of pluralism in which universities are but free markets of opinion in which theology may conceivably function as "one more source of amusement, one more item for curiosity" (106). Neither forensic reason nor the infinite play of desire serves a vision of the university as a place in which positive sciences of diverse kinds collide and, at their best, promote encounter with genuine otherness. Webster proposes that the university ought to be envisaged as a *collegium* of different spheres of intellectual inquiry related by colloquy—not polite conversation of a banal kind, but exchange in which the participants evince both advocacy of their own territory and attentiveness to the territory of others. The implementation of such ideals is clearly challenging and requires theologians to prize spiritual graces, not least the avoidance of *superbia*. Nevertheless, "Christian theology will make its greatest contribution to the conversations of the academy when it pursues Christian difference with an easy conscience and with a measure of determination and doggedness in the face of those who would persuade it to do otherwise" (113). The lecture closes with some reflections on the entailments: the absolute need for theology to pursue its ever-unfinished tasks of self-articulation in exegesis and dogmatics ("There is no such thing as theological capital," 113); the avoidance of timidity concerning the *positum* that is the theologian's concern; the "devastating imperative" of holiness (114); the discontinuity between the transcendent splendor of the gospel and any contingent representation of it in the witness of Christian confession.

Lecture 5, the shortest in the series, revisits the theme of Christian culture's capacity for self-criticism. Webster is again keen to avoid the generic: what matters is not some overall theory of criticism, but what might count as criticism *here*, in the domestic culture of Christian faith. Because it is constituted as it is, by the presence of God in judgment and mercy, the culture of faith contains a "fundamental impulse" that "*subverts* as well as *grounds* the cultural activities which appeal to it" (116). Criticism is not merely imposed from the outside: it is primary to the vocation of the Christian community. The point could be illustrated along almost any major doctrinal trajectory; it is pursued here by appeal to the doctrine of divine revelation. That doctrine is not well mapped in general or comparative terms, where Christian claims about revelatory action are treated as but one instance of a putative revelatory experience in human life and history; nor is it adequately appraised when it is reduced, as so often it has been in modern theology, to an epistemological category, the furnishing of a foundation for belief. Indeed, "The Enlightenment critique of revelation was prepared in some measure by Christian theology itself, when natural philosophy was granted the task of establishing on nontheological grounds the possibility and necessity of revelation" (120). The native soil for the doctrine of revelation is, to the contrary, the particularity of divine self-communication, supremely in Christ by the Spirit, the specific way in which God graciously affords creatures some measure of participation in the boundless self-knowledge that is his. This singular movement is the history of the Triune God's covenant with humanity, a majestic, gratuitous reality in which God makes himself accessible to us but remains mysterious even in his self-disclosure. Over against the mythology of "total critique," demonstrably problematic on a variety of levels, divine revelation as it stands at the center of Christian culture sets a particular standard. The end of critical theological inquiry is "to press the question of the fidelity of all forms of Christian apostolic life, thought, and speech to the revelation of God which projects them into being" (125).

Revelation both *authorizes* and *disturbs*. Theology is but one of the church's critical undertakings (alongside the hearing of the Word and celebration of the sacraments), the church's necessary ways of submitting itself to the judgment of the gospel, a standard "infinitely more searching, radical, and truthful than anything the church could ever generate out of its own resources or by listening to words of criticism directed to it from without" (127). Critical theology is not simply the church setting before itself paradigmatic ideals but its attentiveness to a norm that is "free, personal, and present, and utterly resistant to incorporation" (128). In the end, Christian theology is critical "because of—not despite—the fact that it is a theology of revelation" (128). If critical theology is a mode of reflective attention to the gospel, repentance, humility, and other spiritual virtues are basic to its work.

The final lecture sketches an ethics or, "perhaps better, an *anthropology*" of the theologian (131). The culture of Christian faith requires the cultivation of persons, a costly and indeed at one level impossible affair, dependent entirely upon appeal to God for mercy. "Good theology demands good theologians. . . . Good theologians are those whose life and thought are caught up in the process of being slain and made alive by the gospel and of acquiring and exercising habits of mind and heart which take very seriously the gospel's provocation" (133). Philosophical and educational instincts militate against due integration of scholarship and piety. While the significance of personal formation has helpfully been re-emphasized in some dominant styles of moral and political philosophy, particularly those shaped by neo-Aristotelian accounts of virtue, Christian theology needs to beware of naive ideas of theological education as *simply* a school for character, somehow detached from political forces or the enduring judgment of the gospel. What is being formed in *this* school is "*gospel* character" (136, emphasis added). Because Christian culture is never a steady state, Christian moral psychology is set in the context of human conversion, the transformation and reordering of human life by divine agency. Existence in this region is not "the realization of latent human possibilities, but a *gift*" (140).

Human existence is defined in Christian terms not by what it has been, is, or makes of itself but by what it becomes, as defined forever in the risen Lord Jesus Christ. To be Christian is to have our center not in ourselves but in Christ: to be raised with him and to live in expectation of the consummation of our new life in him. However strange it may seem as a piece of moral psychology, the essence of the life and endeavors of Christian faith lies in "the utter sufficiency of another," and "the life and acts of the believer are wholly taken up by indicating that which he supremely is and does" (142–43). If theological existence is existence in the theater of divine grace, there is "no technology of the Spirit, no moral or intellectual or even spiritual performance which will automatically make us into theologians" (143). At the heart of the theologian's calling, rather, lies *prayer*, the challenging, humble, urgent, intense calling upon God for help: "Prayer underlines the destitution of the theologian when faced with the task of thought and speech of God" (144). Formation and cultivation of the soul have to do, essentially, with waiting on God. In the present situation of Christian theology, the theologian might well seek three things in particular: the fear of God, teachability, and freedom from self-preoccupation. The lecture itself concludes with a prayer.

II

Webster saw *The Culture of Theology* as an attempt to think through the nature of theology's work from the ground up. Questions to do with method, sources, skills, and contexts were familiar to any student of the discipline, but many modern approaches were, he had

come to believe, quite unsatisfactory. Not only did they imply that
contemporary pursuit of the subject consisted in a set of "problems"
guaranteed to vex honest minds; they appeared to assume that such
resolution of the issues as could be had in a complex world was per-
force a matter for present ingenuity. Contemporary theology tended
to exist in essentially uneasy relation to its inheritance, struggling
to work out what to do with Scripture, tradition, and the church's
story, as often as not finding reasons to delimit their pertinence in
favor of present experience. One situation in particular dominated
everything: our place in human cultural history. The assumption was
understandable, and deeply engrained, but deserved to be probed.
Theologians plainly exist in one place rather than another, and cannot avoid its effects. Yet to regard that reality as the main (or only)
determinant of their situation is to suppose that theological work
is—somehow—to be tackled in abstraction from the logic of the
gospel. Why on earth would that be so?

Webster acknowledges in the first lecture that his argument involves "a diagnosis of the current state of the discipline" (44); a good
deal of what he proposes to say will "fly in the face of some of the
prevailing trends of modern theology" (46). As he proceeds, he quips
that some of his hearers might be tempted to write him off as "some
sort of apocalyptic lunatic" (81), or "theologically antediluvian"
(117). The self-depreciation doubtless needs to be seen in its rhetorical context, but there is little question that various "well-entrenched
intellectual conventions in post-Enlightenment Christianity" (47) are
being challenged head-on. Nor are they being tackled as some postmodernists might wish: "However chastened by the genealogists,"
the author remains "unrepentantly (though not, I hope, belligerently)
committed to grand narratives and substance ontology" (47). There
can indeed be no return to the categories of culture or tradition or
reason as detachable from political and social circumstance, or to
texts or learning or virtue abstracted from the dynamics of power.
But the case for Christian difference does not trade on mere relativism
or some philosophy of playful contingency;[6] "severely apophatic"

6. The account of theology within the university in lecture 4 is undoubtedly the
closest the reasoning comes to a pragmatic appeal to intellectual pluralism, not least
because the criteria for what might count as "positive sciences," and the terms upon

accounts of divinity are to be repudiated: the gospel cannot be passed through "the sieve of prior notions of the contingency of all representations" (95). The intellectual and moral potency of theology's descriptive work is convertible into neither "the monologue of instrumental reason" nor "the free play of signs" (114).

If Christian theology is one dimension of living out "amazement" (61), it is seen here as necessarily involving profound disruption of human existence in a fallen world. Webster's argument repeatedly deploys strong language in depiction of that reality. We hear of "the shock of the gospel"; "the comprehensive interruption of all things"; of Jesus Christ as "the great catastrophe of human life and history"; of "God's devastation of human life and history"; of "a kind of loving devastation"; of Christian culture as the place where "God's overthrow of sin attains a special visibility"; of "the sheerly intrusive force" of the presence of the living God among us; and of "astonishment" and "amazement" as vital—and ongoing—aspects of believing response (43, 46, 53, 55, 47, 60–61, 69, 61, 145). The eschatological culture of Christian faith has to do with the presence of that which is "bewilderingly new," an "unmanageable gift"; in the address of the Word, the people of God are "overwhelmed"; Scripture is "a rock thrown in our path, an onslaught which smites our idolatries and us as idolaters"; we are "arrested," "overthrown" (63, 64, 70, 71, 74). The Christian tradition accordingly "subverts"; "the revolution of the gospel" cannot be transformed into equilibrium (93, 94). Again: "There is little that is comfortable about the new creation"; participation in regeneration's "passion" is involved (114). Revelation "comes to do battle with us," to "overthrow" our native blindness, silence, and deafness

which their very diverse practitioners might discern basis for modifying (rather than merely aggregating) their respective investments through attentive engagement with difference, remain inchoate. But even there the aspiration is clearly toward a theological anthropology as a great deal more ambitious than perspectivalism, and the exposition of revelation in lecture 5 moves toward an account of all true knowledge as a matter of divine gift. Whatever else might remain to be said, the difference represented by Christian culture is not, for Webster, to be trivialized—or somehow secured—as merely "one more source of amusement, one more item for curiosity" (106). "Negotiation" of some kind, a "politics of intellectual exchange," will be inevitable in the embodied practices of "consent to conflict" (102–3), but colliding traditions are not merely a "teeming bazaar in which an almost limitless variety of transactions can take place" (94).

concerning the goodness, beauty, and truth of God; it "disturbs" and "accosts" us and "cleaves us apart"; it is the "crisis of Christian life and thought"; it "breaks through our defenses and makes us repent" (123, 75, 125–26). Learning to think and speak well is for the theologian a "bruising business," an acquisition of habits that "shape the soul as it were against the grain"; engagement with God involves experiences of personal growth and change that "inevitably afflict"; the gospel includes a "dispute" with us, and good theologians are "slain" as well as "made alive" by its invasion; it also "destroys"; theologians need to pray as those who "really are in dire straits"; "little progress is possible . . . unless one's will is broken" (131–33, 141, 143–45).

Part of Webster's burden, we might say, is that a great deal of contemporary theology radically underestimates what it means to have dealings with the living God: too many modern theologians, it would seem, have not been disrupted nearly enough.[7] The argument is far more sophisticated than any sledgehammer assault on modernity as such; no golden age is imagined, nor is there wistfulness for an intellectually more manageable world. Fundamental to Webster's case is the insistence that no cultural setting of any such kind can be properly determinative of theology's work, whether as restrictive fate or propitious opportunity; the modern era and all of human history before it are but episodes within a far more significant reality: the business of God's relations with creatures. Modernity itself—a complex construct—is not the primary issue; the complaint is that too much theology has assumed it must be. The instincts of undisturbed reason can be traced in any phase of fallen human existence; they have merely assumed particular forms in a period that has taken its cultural conditions to pose uniquely significant difficulties for

7. Cf. Webster's comment in an essay from the same period: "Theology ought to be frightening, perilous—and not only because, properly undertaken, it ought to issue in intellectual, cultural and spiritual non-conformity, but because the one to whom theology gives its attention is unimaginably demanding." John Webster, "Jesus in Modernity: Reflections on Jüngel's Christology," in John Webster, *Word and Church: Essays in Christian Dogmatics* (Edinburgh and New York: T&T Clark, 2001; 2nd ed., 2016), 151–90, at 188. His commendation of Jüngel's "jaggedness" is prefaced with a citation from Hans Frei: "It is frightening to stand behind a lectern or sit in a comfortable seminar room and talk about Jesus Christ. It is incongruous." Hans Frei, "The Encounter of Jesus with the German Academy," in *Types of Christian Theology* (New Haven: Yale University Press, 1992), 133–46, at 133.

faith—as though history before it was a more hospitable place, or the newness of divine apocalypse was not always quite so new. To think that way is to forget the intrinsically revolutionary nature of the gospel; it is also to lose touch with the attestation of the gospel's potency in the *longue durée* of God's temporal dealings in calling forth and forming a people for his glory.

One evidence of the problem has been the laborious preoccupation of modern (and early-modern) practitioners with the terms upon which theology might possibly be done. In truth, theology is—anytime, anywhere—faith's rational response to an antecedent wonder: "permission and command" are already in place in the actuality of divine revelation (126); "*Whether* there *is* a gospel is a question which has already been answered for theology" (93). A different sign of late-modern malaise has been the thought that divinity eludes us entirely, that the options in practice lie in one form or another of radical negativity, or free or ironic *poiēsis*. Such attitudes are no necessary check on idolatry; they may in fact be quite the reverse, set as they are on imaginative (in-)capacities as norm. In any event, "We may not take a look at the matter of Christian theology as if it could be viewed from a distance, as if we could take up an attitude toward it, even perhaps patronize it with our attention, or maybe simply abandon it at will. Thought and speech about God are propelled into existence by a question posed to us" (145–46). That question is *near*, in the presence of the risen Jesus as contemporary with us in the Spirit's power; there is no distance "to be bridged, as it were, from our end" (87). Nevertheless, the account of revelation foreshadowed in lecture 1 and elaborated in lecture 5 proposes *disturbance* as an essential aspect of the risen one's proximity, in this or any other age; the being who arrives in our midst is ever radically invasive, his Lordship all-comprehensive and all-persistent. Theology cannot settle down or suppose that it is at any point released from absolute obligation to heed his voice. Faith confesses the wonder that he is; obedience involves the continuing recognition of the limitations, the provisional nature, of our best endeavors to speak of his splendor. All this we need to rediscover, and go on learning, if we would duly inhabit the world of Christian existence.

These features serve as very significant qualifiers of what Webster is seeking to offer in "mapping" theology as an element of Christian culture. While on the one hand the terminology seems to echo social-anthropological and moral-philosophical ways of characterizing the practices and habits that define (or ought to define) theology as an aspect of Christian corporate life, on the other, Webster is deeply insistent that what goes on in the space of Christian theology is sui generis. The language of cultural practices cannot be imported wholesale in talking of the nature of Christian theology: *this* culture is unlike any other; its very "ethnography" must itself be "theological" (45; cf. 56). As he sees it, the nature of Christian culture must not be reduced to the description of churchly activities or values, nor can tradition or doctrine or symbol merely be treated as an expression of what a human community has come to generate or idealize. Webster's eschatological and apocalyptic account of culture presses the centrality of divine agency and its irreducible, untamable power.

Theology is an ecclesial task, but the church itself has no being save for the miracle of the divine self-utterance, in all its majestic and sovereign capacity (see 70–71); the church dare not assume the wrong kind of role for itself in the characterization of theology's work. Theologians are what they are and do what they do in consequence of the purposes and actions of the Triune God, who alone generates, enables, and rules over their endeavors. The intellectual, spiritual, and moral responsibilities of the territory in which they are placed are real indeed, but their works as such are always subject to the judgment of the divine presence that precedes and encloses them. Webster is concerned to avoid docetism (see, e.g., 54), to recognize the essential historical and social embodiment of the Christian community, its texts and traditions, and to steer away from idealism (46). But he is insistent that theology's culture is never merely "made" by us in any straightforward sense, for "there is no point at which God's action retires in favor of human undertakings" (54). Theologians inhabit a space in which they have been set, acting out roles and fulfilling tasks to which they have been appointed, "and doing so with an energy which is God's own gift" (54). Their situation, activities, and obligations cannot be reduced to one more representation of moral behavior or social practice.

The author is conscious that his account may well appear "exotic" (53; 99) or "utopian" (59; 100–101). Sections of the argument—most notably lecture 6, and parts of lectures 2, 3, and 4—include specific advice, but even in its second half the series is a long way removed from any facile prescription for busy pragmatists. In offering a horizon against which to consider present practices, to adjudge the ways in which these may have become habituated to operating in either anxious or prideful disregard of the God of the gospel,[8] Webster proposes something quite different from the favored styles of contemporary theology—far too often nervous where it ought to be bold, complacent where it ought to repent. The evangel's categorical indicatives are liberating and all-demanding all at once, and primordial to any formulation of the tasks to which theology is summoned in its concrete situations. In all this there is a substantial challenge to prevalent instincts to head straight to answers in which ecclesial culture might take its cues from the world rather than the Word.

Webster would later consider such reasoning defensive and unduly contrastive, its content not yet—for all its ambition—doctrinal enough, the restrictions a symptom of the circumstances in which he found himself working at this stage in his career. To this we shall return. But it is important here that such defensiveness as the lectures do evince is not overstated. They are clearly intended to set forth a strongly positive account of their theme, indeed to free theologians from the inhibitions and false burdens associated with other approaches.[9] Amid the fierce talk of crisis and devastation lie unmistakable notes of boldness and joy. The world of new creation is a place brought into being by divine arrival in our midst, an entrance that is certainly a "shock" of vast proportions, but also the greatest of good news (43–44, 46); theology is undertaken in the presence of the one whose saving and transforming reality is contemporary and gracious, redirecting us to "the true ends of [our] human flourishing" (145). There is "delight" in the theologian's testimony (43, 96, 145), and in her reading of Scripture as the *viva vox Dei* (64). No small aspect of theology's work in its descriptive or didactic modes is the praise of God (93). The orderly repetition of Holy Scripture involves our edification

---

8. The classical "marks" of the church are invoked in somewhat similar terms in lecture 5 (116–17).

9. Including, notably, the false restrictions generated by fixation with their own particular instantiations of the tradition (see lecture 6, 147).

as creatures, the promotion of "fidelity to the gospel which gives life" (93). Part of Webster's endeavor to present the task of theology as he does is a quest to depict its culture as a realm in which human existence is set free from falsehood and vanity, restored to its proper dignity and fulfillment. Theologians are continually overwhelmed and undone; they are also being invited here to recover a sense of the privilege of their calling, the immensity of its resources, and the magnificence of its prospects in "a future which is God's" (54).

III

What had led Webster to think about Christian theology in these kinds of terms? The matter was quite personal. Trained in Cambridge in the later 1970s, he had come fairly early to feel that his theological education had been obsessed with doctrinal criticism to the detriment of constructive theology; there had been no shortage of talk about method, but the approach had been dominated by the perceived imperatives of intellectual context, the enduring analysis of what it might (or might not) be feasible to say about particular bits of classical doctrine under the conditions of modernity. To that end, theology had sought assistance from other fields—philosophy, history, social theory, occasionally the natural sciences—but had seldom evinced much confidence in being *itself*. There had been little positive vision of Christian doctrine as a whole—its relationship to scriptural exegesis, the range and depth of its expression in Christian tradition, the nature of its intellectual, spiritual, and moral roles within the church's life. In the unquestioned valorization of general inquiry and the unqualified determinacy of present sociocultural location, catechesis had been devalued; history was burden as much as gift. The results were theologically and spiritually slender: an analysis, adjustment, or correlation of classical confession rather than participation in its delight. Webster's graduate work on Eberhard Jüngel[10] had taken him into richer territory, but in his earliest academic

---

10. John B. Webster, "Distinguishing between God and Man: Aspects of the Theology of Eberhard Jüngel" (PhD diss., University of Cambridge, 1982). A more

teaching he had—as he later saw it, at least—only gradually felt his way out of the instincts of uneasy relation to the tradition and into a clearer sense of positive Christian dogmatics as "a wise, edifying and joyful science."[11]

That vocation had been clarified considerably in his years in Canada (1986–96), where he had come to teach theology in overtly confessional terms and found fresh stimulus in an ecumenical setting. He had been influenced in particular by a Jesuit colleague, George Schner, with whom he shared a graduate seminar. Trained at Yale, Schner had imbibed much from the instincts of his postliberal teachers and was skilled in tracing nineteenth- and twentieth-century theology's complex debts to the assumptions of modernity; "a master reader,"[12] he had helped Webster to plot the genealogies of revisionist and correlationist approaches and find remedy for their consequences in Protestant and Roman Catholic divinity: doctrine and exegesis had rich resources of their own; accommodations born of cultural anxiety were not the only intelligent options.[13] Webster had absorbed a good deal of so-called "Yale" theology; he had also gone on working intensely on Barth. Postliberal accounts of Scripture, ecclesiology, and ethics remained impressive, and had learned important things from Barth; they had also underestimated Barth's investment in the antecedent freedom and abundance of God as basic to the significance of creaturely sociality and action. Postliberal thinkers were by no means always culpable of the crasser forms of reductionism or relativism alleged by their critics, but Webster's judgment was that they placed too much emphasis on theology as a form of religious life or sociolinguistic activity; features of human practice as much as divine agency and purpose seemed the primary markers of Christian

---

spacious assessment followed in J. B. Webster, *Eberhard Jüngel: An Introduction to His Theology* (Cambridge: Cambridge University Press, 1986; 2nd ed. 1991).

11. John Webster, "Discovering Dogmatics," in *Shaping a Theological Mind: Theological Context and Methodology*, ed. Darren C. Marks (Aldershot and Burlington, VT: Ashgate, 2002), 129–36, at 130.

12. John Webster, "Introduction: Philosophy and the Practices of Christianity," in *George P. Schner: Essays Catholic and Critical*, ed. Philip G. Ziegler and Mark Husbands (Aldershot and Burlington, VT: Ashgate, 2003), xi–xix, at xi.

13. On the influences of Catholic thinkers on Webster's work in general and his range of debts and critical interactions, see Fergus Kerr, "John Webster and Catholic Theology," *New Blackfriars* 98 (2017): 457–81.

distinctiveness.[14] That was a problem. Webster's work on Barth's ethics had enabled him to trace out major aspects of an alternative: divine aseity did not devalue the moral density of creatures; it funded it in the right currency.[15]

Webster had also begun to set out some of his thoughts on what it meant for theology to engage its inheritance in general. In his inaugural lecture in 1995 as Ramsay Armitage Professor of Systematic Theology at Wycliffe College, Toronto, he had taken as his theme "Reading Theology."[16] Arguing that theologians must take seriously the "textual deposit" of the Christian tradition, howsoever unfashionable traditioned inquiry may have come to be, he emphasized that theology ought to be vitally concerned with exegesis and catechesis. *Reading* was simply basic to theological education—supremely the reading of Scripture, but also the reading of the classics of Christian response to Scripture. Webster argued for what he called (with debts to Jüngel) "a theological account of theology."[17] Theology could primarily be not an act of intellectual construction, but a means by which the church is summoned to remain faithful to the gospel. Theology serves the church by drawing its attention to the Word of God as manifest in Holy Scripture. To that end, hearing the Word is fundamental. Through engagement with the history of its reception, theology also underscores the distance between Scripture and tradition, the fact that the church's representations of the gospel are ever contingent and open to correction by the Word. Theology thus operates both in a descriptive or locative fashion, helping the church to articulate its identity and message, and in a utopian mode, helping the church to resist "cultural sclerosis."[18]

14. See John Webster, "Theology after Liberalism?," in *Theology after Liberalism: A Reader*, ed. John Webster and George P. Schner (Oxford and Malden, MA: Blackwell, 2000), 52–64.

15. See in particular John Webster, *Barth's Ethics of Reconciliation* (Cambridge: Cambridge University Press, 1995); *Barth's Moral Theology: Human Action in Barth's Thought* (Edinburgh: T&T Clark; Grand Rapids: Eerdmans, 1998).

16. John Webster, "Reading Theology," *Toronto Journal of Theology* 13 (1997): 53–63.

17. Cf., e.g., Eberhard Jüngel, *God as the Mystery of the World: On the Foundation of the Theology of the Crucified One in the Dispute between Theism and Atheism* (Grand Rapids: Eerdmans, 1983), 4.

18. Webster, "Reading Theology," 61.

"Theological theology" was the theme to which Webster returned in his inaugural lecture as Oxford's Lady Margaret Professor of Divinity in October 1997.[19] A contrast is drawn between theology as it had typically come to be practiced in the modern research university and theology as it might be done. The anthropology of inquiry generally operative in modern university culture sees the most basic acts of the reflective self as representative and judgmental: we summon the world into our presence in order to assess it. Such *wissenschaftlich* principles have been heavily promoted to generic status as academic ideals, and with that move, formation (*Bildung*) has been downplayed. The quest for universal protocols for intellectual practice has historically come to be shared by theology itself, which from early-modern times—if not well before—has come to trade heavily in the coinage of supposedly general principles of reason and knowledge. The motivations have varied, but in all of it theology has come to evince internal disorder as much as capitulation to external pressures; losing sight of its proper subject matter and procedures, or suffering a failure of nerve in regard to their deployment, the subject has become "de-regionalized," increasingly marginal as a serious field of inquiry capable of contributing substantially to the discourse of the academy or indeed the edification of the church. What is needed is frank recovery of theology as the articulation of Christian *difference*. Theology flourishes when it is confident in its own resources, not anxious to find its materials elsewhere or conform itself to other norms. Such an approach means inevitable challenge for the university, but also real contribution: theologians may begin to model a different kind of intellectual life and thus commend attention to the God whose priority and plenitude are the transcendent source of all true wisdom.

Several of the emphases in "Reading Theology" and "Theological Theology" are echoed in *The Culture of Theology*, and there is evidence of Webster's refrains in the period: the primacy of God as self-revealing subject; the location of theology within the dynamics of

19. John Webster, *Theological Theology: An Inaugural Lecture Delivered before the University of Oxford on 28 October 1997* (Oxford: Clarendon, 1998), reprinted as John Webster, "Theological Theology," in *Confessing God: Essays in Christian Dogmatics II* (New York: T&T Clark, 2005; 2nd ed., 2016), 11–31.

God's action to reconcile and perfect estranged creatures; the nature of texts, traditions, and community as instruments of that purpose; the responsibility of theologians to listen humbly to the Word set forth in Scripture, to recognize the gifts given in the church's history of confession, and to be modest about their own little acts of reception and testimony; the critical functions of theology in the due inhabitation of ministerial roles in the church and in the world. The eschatological and apocalyptic accents in the Burns Lectures are in obvious ways reminiscent of the early Barth, evoked in the opening address,[20] and Barth remains a pervasive influence. Kant appears as something of a recurring foil; Jüngel is present as might be expected; Calvin and Kierkegaard are invoked to make important points; Augustine reminds us of the dispositions of the theologian, not least the need for prayer.

The influences of postliberal discourse are clear: "culture" as an overarching category; the practices and traditions of the church in its "sphere" or "space" or "region"; the regulative and intra-systemically critical functions of Christian doctrine; the inhabitation of textual worlds; the relationship of public and private; the work of rhetoric and action as moral testimony. Hans Frei, David Kelsey, George Lindbeck, Ronald Thiemann, Kathryn Tanner, and others appear, in nuanced terms. Roman Catholic references are relatively sparse. As the decline narrative of "Theological Theology" also illustrates, Webster appreciates that the discipline, its materials, and its practices are ever embedded in a host of social, political, and cultural forces; yet as he sees it, the problem has often been not that theology has failed to keep pace with its wider intellectual environment but that it has kept pace with it all too well.[21] Against that calibration, protest is in order. Webster repudiates the hubris of the Enlightenment's putative universalities; he insists on particularity, urges respect for inheritances, cherishes meaningful rather than vacuous "conversations" with otherness. At the same time, the case for "Christianness" and "nonconformity" involves, as we have noted, much more than mere critique of the modern; the quarrel is not with the obvious

20. Cf. also the equation of the eschatological gospel with Kierkegaard's "paradox-religion" in lecture 3 (96–97).
21. Cf. Webster, "Theological Theology," in Webster, *Confessing God*, 23.

reality that theology faces contemporary challenges, but with the assumptions upon which they are met. All this attests the influences of thinkers concerned to move on from classical liberalism and its etiolation of theology's beauty.

The Culture of Theology was written fairly quickly, over a few weeks. Its range of reference is quite carefully controlled (in lesser hands, the critical case might readily have been overtaken by polemic), but there is some quite notable allusion to modern philosophy, social and critical theory, the study of religion, hermeneutics, and ethics. Webster is keen to speak seriously to an academic audience; he is aware that the kind of theology he is seeking to commend needs to be marked out carefully, particularly in a university setting. Devotees of standard practices might have found reasons to rethink some of their assumptions in view of intellectual arguments advanced elsewhere, but old habits died hard; whether cautious or whimsical, skeptical or expressive, plenty of contemporary theology appeared stuck on a diet of moralism, or determined to talk about anything other than the contours of its confession. Much of it sounded as if nothing much had happened to the paradigms of foundationalism; yet these had—of course—been subject to critique on many fronts. Contextual theologies—an undoubted enthusiasm for some of his initial hearers—knew better on that score at least but ran into problems on others. Principled postmodern approaches—where they involved a repudiation of the metaphysics of presence or history or identity in favor of ironic detachment or imaginative play—might be exercises in one form or another of self-indulgence. Webster's position is unabashedly other to all of this. The polemical edge can hardly be missed; yet it is, on the whole, deployed with measure, an element of the work rather than its governing register. Some sharp things are said about the mistakes of modern theology and biblical studies, but there is no crude taxonomy of all the relevant errors or fierce assaults on their present-day exemplars. The same is true of the wider intellectual correspondence. The case could hardly be described as apologetic; much of its drift is precisely the opposite. Still, it is the argument of one who knows that theology need not always blush in learned company, even as it insists on its distinctiveness, and that it ought to be able to converse intelligently and charitably with other spheres of inquiry. Some of the interactions here are—very courteously—provocative; others are quite happy to recognize degrees of common cause: on the deconstruction of universal rationality, or the importance of tradition-constituted inquiry, or the practices of responsible textual reading, or the place of formation. Whatever their cast, the engagements are not, for their time, less than informed; they serve to illustrate the principle that theology need not be "too anxious about its standing vis-à-vis other disciplines, especially its near neighbors in history and philosophy" (51).

The later Webster showed much less interest in appeal to such resources; indeed, he felt there was a certain danger in the practice: if the theologian's responsibilities are not reducible to a task set by philosophical critique or cultural studies, the application of genealogy or polemic deserves to be kept under strict control, lest theological language lose the specificity it demands. Webster's work never would be intellectually narrow (it continued to be shaped by remarkably wide reading and knew far more capacity than some supposed to engage across boundaries), but he would frame his accounts of theology, church, and university in more explicitly doctrinal terms still, the assets drawn from the history of salvation much more than the history of ideas. Such moves were arguably a (more?) logical application of the conviction expressed in the lectures that theology's situation deserves to be appraised in spiritual and moral as much as intellectual registers and ought not to be dominated by the wrong kinds of reference-point. There never would be some coarse argument that philosophy did not matter, whether as critic or as ally, only that its concerns ought not to wield control, for theology has another crucial story to tell: "If our intellects are depraved, it is not because we are children of Scotus or Descartes or Kant, but because we are children of Adam."[22] Webster would come to think that a doctrinal narrative of creation, fall, and redemption actually serves to say more, not less, about the significance of intellectual life outside of the church and its culture; to foreground divine action even more strongly is in fact to speak better of human intelligence and its achievements.

22. John Webster, "On the Theology of the Intellectual Life," in John Webster, *God without Measure: Working Papers in Christian Theology*, vol. 2: *Virtue and Intellect* (New York: Bloomsbury T&T Clark, 2016), 141–56, at 147.

The spread of his resources in this text is, however, indicative of his intellectual situation and aims at the time.

Toronto had for Webster been an environment in which academic and churchly activities came together quite fruitfully; Oxford, for all its opportunities, was already proving more challenging, a setting in which Barth studies, dogmatics, and theologically ambitious reading of the Bible encountered bemused observers or principled critics as much as eager devotees. There were plenty of gifted students to teach, from a range of confessional backgrounds; the chair to which he had been appointed was then still reserved for an Anglican priest, a canonry of Christ Church went with the role, and service to the church remained a regular aspect of his work.[23] Yet "a measure of academic isolation" was already his experience, and he was distinctly cautious about optimistic assessments of the contemporary state of systematic theology, especially in Britain.[24] The arguments in the Burns Lectures were themselves presented in a self-consciously pluralist setting, which had known debates of its own about the relationship of secular academy and church and about the obligations of the church to its traditions. If theology's capacity to function well in such contexts was to be evident, a great deal more than anxious conservatism or fideism was required; to see the strategy proposed by Webster as retreatist or merely nostalgic is perverse.[25] Nevertheless, it would be in the faithful enactment of its proper identity, not the attempt to render that identity in some other form, that theology would bear intellectual and moral testimony of a kind that might actually make the academy notice and might remind the church also of what it ought to be about.

Even so, moving on from liberalism could not mean appropriation of alternatives that risked the reduction of dogmatics to interpretative theory, or the hyperinflation of ecclesiology. Much effort is expended to render an—essentially Reformed—account

23. Some examples of his preaching in the period can be found in John Webster, *Confronted by Grace: Meditations of a Theologian* (Bellingham, WA: Lexham, 2015), previously published as John Webster, *The Grace of Truth* (Farmington Hills, MI: Oil Lamp Books, 2011).

24. Webster, "Discovering Dogmatics," 133; also Webster, *Word and Church*, 6.

25. See, e.g., lecture 3 (92–93); lecture 6 (146–47); and the whole tenor of the argument about the nature of divine revelation and criticism in lectures 1 and 5.

of the Christian community as established, sustained, and ruled by divine agency, and the recurrent theological motifs are clear: the resurrection of Jesus Christ; his free and lordly self-movement toward us in the power of the Spirit; his contemporaneity with us and living eloquence; the inseparability of divine revelation from the doctrine of the Triune God; the right "kind" of transcendence, in which God in his majesty is known and confessed though never domesticated; the divine use of Holy Scripture as authority over the church and instrument of Christian sanctification; the apostolicity of the church as divinely generated. For Webster, the church must not be confounded with Christ himself, nor is Christ reliant upon the church to body forth his presence in the world. Theology as an act of witness is, in a vital sense, liberated as well as impelled by that reality.

Barth indubitably helped to shape the enthusiasms; as Barth had recognized, the relationship between theologians and their Lord might be stated simply: "Everything that is to be said of the church is said by saying: 'We point to him'" (92).[26] Ongoing close work on Barth[27] continued to steer Webster well away from what he took to be grandiose accounts of church and ministry, or merely narratival renditions of Christian identity; theology's location was within the constitutive history of God's creating, reconciling, and perfecting works. Postliberal voices enriched, but there was no uncritical assimilation of their discourse; the legacy of Barth continued to press important correctives. In three keynote addresses at a conference in Melbourne in December 1998, a few months after his Dunedin lectures, Webster set out a memorable depiction of Barth's distinctively dogmatic account of realism in confrontation with one version or another of "postmodernism"; the closing note was an appeal to learn afresh from Barth that no philosophical context compels the

26. Evoking Karl Barth, *Church Dogmatics* IV/3 (Edinburgh: T&T Clark, 1961), 797. On the nature of faithful attestation, see the short essay from the same period, John Webster, "What Is the Gospel?," in *Grace and Truth in a Secular Age*, ed. Timothy Bradshaw (Grand Rapids: Eerdmans, 1998), 109–18; quite a few of the emphases there resonate with themes developed in lectures 1 and 3 in particular.

27. Resulting inter alia in John Webster, *Barth* (New York: Continuum, 2000; 2nd ed., 2004; 3rd ed., 2015); John Webster, ed., *The Cambridge Companion to Karl Barth* (Cambridge: Cambridge University Press, 2000).

church's "intellectual recapitulation," so long as the gospel's habits of mind are retained: whatever the setting, "good, fruitful and edifying theology [remains] theological theology, done as if nothing had happened."[28] The same period also brought further insistence on the need for a robustly doctrinal treatment of scriptural interpretation and a concern to push firmly away from hermeneutics as general science.[29] There was a world of difference between obedient listening to the voice of God in Holy Scripture and any mere celebration of "textuality," or the elaboration of basically transferable interpretative conventions. To speak of the particularity of Christian intellectual and moral activity required, in turn, much more than a description of its social distinctiveness in human terms. The operative role of divine agency in the due reception of Scripture, as well as in its generation and sanctification, was crucial; otherwise, readerly acts and churchly decisions assumed the wrong significance. Deficiency in this area, as evidenced by "the recent luxuriant growth of ecclesial ethics,"[30] remained a real burden; the language of habit or practice or virtue or conversation could readily be overplayed, and excessive investment in social or political context was only one expression of the problem. Discerning theologians may have understood the problems of correlationism, but where an essential language concerning God's revelatory self-presence was "occluded or accorded only background status," the disposition of doctrines might still seem closer to Schleiermacher than to Barth (85).

28. John Webster, "Barth and Postmodern Theology: A Fruitful Confrontation?," in *Karl Barth: A Future for Postmodern Theology?*, ed. Geoff Thompson and Christiaan Mostert (Hindmarsh, SA: Australian Theological Forum, 2000), 1–69, at 69. These addresses offer an important expansion on some of Webster's assumptions in the context of the Burns Lectures in regard to theology and history, as well as on his sense of how one might begin to elaborate a Christian theological anthropology as an exercise in gospel-constituted humanism; on the latter, see also a slightly later essay: John Webster, "The Human Person," in *The Cambridge Companion to Postmodern Theology*, ed. Kevin J. Vanhoozer (Cambridge: Cambridge University Press, 2003), 219–34.

29. See, e.g., John Webster, "Hermeneutics in Modern Theology: Some Doctrinal Reflections," *Scottish Journal of Theology* 51 (1998): 307–41, reprinted in Webster, *Word and Church*, 47–86; the paper was read to a seminar at the University of Otago in August 1998.

30. John Webster, "Christ, Church, and Reconciliation," in Webster, *Word and Church*, 211–30, at 214.

The quest to avoid "moral agonistics" certainly ought not to force the wrong kinds of distinctions between divine and human action: that was, ironically, to repeat modernity's mistakes rather than hear the gospel's declaration.[31] Nevertheless, theology's work was not to become fixated on human tasks of moral or aesthetic representation to the world; too often, especially in the discipline's most conversational modes, it seemed to be so. Even where systematic theology was seeking to be constructive in its dialogues with contemporary culture, no longer taken up with the tired projects of critical justification but eager to discern the voice of God in the world at large, its ventures might still amount to one form or another of "soft correlationism chastened by bits of Barth," or—Radical Orthodoxy presumably in the sights—an "over-clever Anglo-Catholicism with precious little Christology, soteriology or pneumatology."[32] Celebrations of polyphony in theological method all too readily forgot that the resources of other realms might bear restrictive covenants. The theologian's acts of intellectual testimony could scarcely be ventured in insularity, but the fidelity of their witness was also intimately connected with the theologian's focus: that in turn obliged "a kind of ascesis, a laying aside, an *inattention* to all sorts of stimuli."[33] If theology's fundamental burden was devotion to a particular canon of texts—Holy Scripture at its center, the greater and lesser commentaries of the Christian tradition ranged around that—faithful testimony meant glad invocation of the church's confession of the Word, not the potential relativization of that confession's density amid a welter of other interests. Vital things flowed from appropriation of the point: deliverance from the implication that theology's speech about the gospel is merely an elevated social or moral project; repudiation of the idea that divine presence is either vaguely diffused everywhere or somehow coextensive with ecclesial energies.

As the Burns Lectures themselves imply, Webster was conscious of the risks of being cast—as he would put it elsewhere—in the role of "a theological Ishmael," one living over against all his kin (Gen.

---

31. Webster, *Word and Church*, 213.

32. Webster, "Discovering Dogmatics," 133; cf. Webster, *Word and Church*, 6.

33. John Webster, "Article Review: David F. Ford: *Self and Salvation*," *Scottish Journal of Theology* 54 (2001): 548–59, at 559.

16:12).[34] But serious dogmatics mattered immensely, and the resources of the past had, as Barth himself—or indeed the great theologians of *ressourcement*—discerned, so much to offer. Together with Colin Gunton of King's College, London, Webster would establish the *International Journal of Systematic Theology* as a further outlet for the endeavors.[35]

Webster's deep concerns with the place of texts and traditions and the nature of the discipline in directly theological terms took him a great deal further. The early 2000s saw him work much more on the relationship between theology and Scripture, generating, among other fruits, his *Scottish Journal of Theology* lectures at Aberdeen in 2001, published as *Holy Scripture: A Dogmatic Sketch*.[36] His abiding interest in the characterization of the tasks of theological thinking and the purposes of God in forming the theologian was also evident in an introductory account of theology, in a short series of lectures on holiness, as an activity of "holy reason."[37] The emphasis there on the need to locate the theological task within the divine economy was suggestive of a growing sense that it was inadequate merely to say theology operates with a different anthropology of inquiry, or as the activity of those who have been interrupted; it was necessary to spell this matter out quite fully. Inasmuch as the moral ontology of all human agents is established by their relation to God, and creaturely being is determined by the moral history enacted between God and creatures, the work of theologians is set specifically within the story of redemption, the great process by which the fallen and the estranged are in sovereign mercy brought to know and love the God for whom they are made; the basis of that entire history is God himself. Scripture and reason must be considered in this context. Scripture is the chief textual instrument of God's revelatory and

34. Webster, *Word and Church*, 6.

35. See John Webster, "Editorial," *International Journal of Systematic Theology* 1 (1999): 1–3.

36. John Webster, *Holy Scripture: A Dogmatic Sketch* (Cambridge: Cambridge University Press, 2003). Various themes from the Burns Lectures are expanded; lecture 1 is referenced at 124n43.

37. John Webster, *Holiness* (London: SCM; Grand Rapids: Eerdmans, 2003); the material was first presented in 2002 as the Day-Higginbotham Lectures at Southwestern Baptist Theological Seminary, Fort Worth, Texas.

redemptive purpose, an embassy of his eloquence, directed toward the regeneration of its readers as they encounter his Word in inspired and sanctified human speech. Theological reason is creaturely intelligence under renovation, redirected by grace to its purposed end in fellowship with God.

Many of these moves had already been signaled in the Burns Lectures, but they came to be stated in both more expansive and more careful terms. Webster's transition to the University of Aberdeen in 2003 took him into an environment in which he felt freer, and initiated a period of significant productivity in dogmatics.[38] There was an undoubted broadening of his resources: more patristic and medieval material, yet more of the Reformed tradition, and far greater nuance with it. Thomas in particular came to assume steadily higher profile in his work. Several core instincts did not disappear: there was an essential distinction between created and uncreated being; revelation was inseparable from the personal movement of the God who elects, reconciles, and perfects (there could be no pre-theological prolegomena to theology); the gospel was in a deep sense "*separate*," never merely identifiable with the church or theological reason, incapable of assimilation as "an element—even a founding element—of an ecclesial or intellectual culture."[39] Webster increasingly came to believe, however, that if the history of God and creatures was indeed the central context for understanding theology's situation, then some of the sharp contrasts developed in his earlier work were unhelpful. Rather than focusing on the interruptive force of the gospel as such, he sought more and more to trace the events that the gospel declares back to their essential basis in the doctrine of God; rather than merely drawing a thick distinction between the culture of faith and other forms of human existence, he aspired to identify the ground of that distinction, and the ground of all forms of creaturely reality, in the nature of God's relations with the world.

38. Some examples are collected in Webster, *Confessing God*, though that work also contains essays from Oxford; and John Webster, *The Domain of the Word: Scripture and Theological Reason* (New York: T&T Clark, 2012). In 2007 *The Oxford Handbook of Systematic Theology* (Oxford: Oxford University Press) was published, coedited with Kathryn Tanner and Iain Torrance.

39. Webster, *Confessing God*, 5.

Webster's writing expressed, with growing depth and range, "a discovery of the content and consequences of Christian teaching about God's perfection."[40] The "eschatological register" expressed in some of the Oxford work—and not least, surely, in the Burns Lectures—was born of "unease about, even alienation from" an intellectual environment; it reflected "a reaction (over-reaction?) to historical naturalism."[41] Theology's setting, like every creaturely reality, stood in relation to the God whose inner perfection and blessedness are the ground of his creative, communicative, preserving, and restoring presence—wholly gracious, free, and good, "the inexhaustibly full animating principle of created life and movement."[42]

Webster continued to evince deep interest in the architectonics of systematic theology—in the scope and proportions of doctrines, their interrelations and order. In addition to the emphases on resurrection, ascension, and the miracle of revelation, as sketched under Barth's influence in the Burns Lectures, we come to hear much more of the perfect God who fashions, cares for, reconciles, and perfects creatures, and whose history with them is the magnificent, free overflow of his eternal, wholly realized relational life in himself; the accents were drawn increasingly from premodern Western theology. Trinity and creation came to form a somewhat more dominant pairing than Trinity and Christology. The matchless name of Jesus Christ and his incomparable achievement remained the "resplendent center" of reality as declared by the gospel,[43] but soteriology as such, even the definitive work of the eternal Son incarnate, did not sum up or norm all doctrine. The gospel's good news needed to be set within an overall account of the Triune God's *opera exeuntia*, commencing with the transitive acts of his goodness which effect creation itself and going on to speak of all that the creator subsequently does in providence, redemption, and consummation to outwork his invincible ends. The entire narrative of nature and of grace derived from God's eternal

40. Webster, *Confessing God*, ix (preface to the 2016 edition).

41. Webster, *Word and Church*, xi (preface to the 2016 edition).

42. Webster, *Confessing God*, x (preface to the 2016 edition).

43. John Webster, "Prolegomena to Christology: Four Theses," in *The Person of Christ*, ed. Stephen R. Holmes and Murray A. Rae (New York: T&T Clark, 2005), 19–36, at 25, reprinted in Webster, *Confessing God*, 131–49, at 137.

plenitude, the essential source of all our blessing: "The fully realized character of God's life in himself [deserved to be] acknowledged as the first truth of Christian teaching and so as an operative principle in any passage of theological thought."[44]

In the last decade of his work, in Aberdeen until the summer of 2013 then all too briefly in St. Andrews, Webster increasingly sought to present this specific kind of relationship between God and creatures as crucial: first theology, then economy. To get the matter right was not at all to downplay creatureliness or history or the processes of knowledge outside of Christian confession—it was to view all these things *better*: as "pure benefit, intelligible only as God is known and loved in his inherent completeness."[45] To speak first of God in himself, then of God in his outer works, continued to mean profound reordering of pervasive contemporary instincts, both formally and materially, such as theologians' diverse ways of collapsing being and time, or overstating creaturely mediation, or implying that God is somehow a magnified agent on the same plane as other agents. But emphasis on divine perfection, as another important series of lectures in 2007 explored, also meant the glory of the presence of God with us, the temporal missions of Christ and the Spirit and their comprehensive consequences.[46] The doctrine of God was foundational for a proper account of creaturely dignity, its moral enactment, and ends. "*Because* dogmatics inquires into God, it inquires also into God's outer works, considering not only their grounds in the divine will and processions but also their temporal forms and effects. *Accordingly*, dogmatics is required to give its attention not only to God the creator and his acts of creation, but also to creatures, their natures and properties, and especially to the human creature."[47]

44. Webster, *Confessing God*, ix (preface to the 2016 edition).

45. John Webster, "*Omnia . . . pertractantur in sacra doctrina sub ratione Dei*: On the Matter of Christian Theology," in *God without Measure: Working Papers in Christian Theology*, vol. 1: *God and the Works of God* (New York: Bloomsbury T&T Clark, 2016), 3–11, at 6.

46. John Webster, "Perfection and Presence: God with Us, according to the Christian Confession," Kantzer Lectures, Trinity Evangelical Divinity School, Deerfield, IL, September 2007. A revision of the lectures for publication was incomplete at the time of his death; the recordings of the original addresses are available at henrycenter.tiu.edu.

47. John Webster, "Introduction: *Agere sequitur esse*," in Webster, *God without Measure*, vol. 2, 1–4, at 2.

Thus emerged much more spacious accounts of intellect and virtue, including some of the dispositions and habits commended in lecture 6 here, and of what it means to be slain and made alive in Christ by the Spirit: the fear of God, patience, humility, docility, good and bad speech, the theology of the intellectual life.[48] There would be much more of the language of "contemplation," reflective of patristic, medieval, and Puritan influences, and much more on the reordering of desires. Thomas, not mentioned at all in *The Culture of Theology*, played a crucial role in much of it. There would be clarification that curiosity as such is not a virtue: "studiousness" is.[49] There would be a much fuller (and ultimately less relativist) construal of the place of theology in the university,[50] and an outstanding meditation on intellectual patience in which Webster explores, as "one of the chief parts of divinity's apostolic office in the university," its calling to articulate "a metaphysics and morals of intellectual inquiry, presenting and enacting a version of the good intellectual life."[51]

Further reading had undoubtedly moved things on; there was obvious evidence of what it meant to venture beyond Barth and Jüngel to older resources. Earlier overstatements and misjudgments of diverse kinds would in humility be corrected: a negative evaluation of the relationship between God, revelation, and Scripture in post-Reformation divinity (cf., e.g., 70); an inadequate exposition of the nature of the inspiration of Scripture as text and of the diverse ways

48. See esp. Webster, *God without Measure*, vol. 2, chaps. 7–11.

49. Cf. John Webster, "Curiosity," in *Theology and Human Flourishing: Essays in Honor of Timothy J. Gorringe*, ed. Mike Higton, Jeremy Law, and Christopher Rowland (Eugene, OR: Cascade, 2011), 212–23, reprinted in Webster, *Domain of the Word*, 193–202, with lecture 4, esp. 110–13; though note also lecture 6, 145.

50. John B. Webster, "God, Theology, Universities," in *Indicative of Grace— Imperative of Freedom: Essays in Honour of Eberhard Jüngel in His 80th Year*, ed. R. David Nelson (New York: Bloomsbury T&T Clark, 2014), 241–54, reprinted in Webster, *God without Measure*, vol. 2, 157–72. See also John Webster, "*Regina Artium*: Theology and the Humanities," in *Theology, University, Humanities: Initium Sapientiae Timor Domini*, ed. Christopher Craig Brittain and Francesca Aran Murphy (Eugene, OR: Cascade, 2011), 39–63, reprinted in Webster, *Domain of the Word*, 173–92.

51. John Webster, "Intellectual Patience," in Webster, *God without Measure*, vol. 2, 173–87, at 176.

in which Scripture functions within the economy of the Spirit's action in the illumination and sanctification of the saints. In important papers such as "Biblical Reasoning" (2008)[52] and "Principles of Systematic Theology" (2009),[53] Webster sketched with great clarity the relationship of Scripture, reason, and fellowship with the God whose primordial purpose it is to grant creatures a share in his boundless self-knowledge. The authority of God's self-giving was seen as vital to the relationship between gospel and church: the situation in which the church exists—some of the spatial language would persist—is the sphere or domain of the living Lordship of the risen Christ by the Spirit; the living reality of his rule, exercised through the instrumentality of Holy Scripture, is fundamental.

The mature Webster felt that the vision of "theological theology" set out in his Oxford inaugural lecture in particular was inadequate, an unsatisfactory combination of the reactionary and the defensive. Theology is "theological," he would argue, inasmuch as it attends to its proper object, namely God and all things relative to God; the principles, ends, and virtues of the theologian must be specified accordingly. The *kinds* of conversation that theology can broker will be more interesting, more radical, and more generative for the academy if they are located in a more robust and expansive account of Trinity, creation, and redemption.[54] Divine metaphysics as such was even more important than had earlier been set forth; the divine names and attributes were crucial; a transcendent (never merely symbolic or exemplarist) Christology mattered profoundly; the Holy Spirit had indeed an identifiably distinct role alongside the risen and ascended Son as the completing agent of the divine resolve to be known. Bibliology continued to be prior to hermeneutics, but tracing how the nature and interpretation of Scripture were to be treated as corollaries of God's relation to history and creatures (and thus located within a theology of Word and church) meant the metaphysics of nature,

52. John Webster, "Biblical Reasoning," *Anglican Theological Review* 90 (2008): 733–51, reprinted in Webster, *Domain of the Word*, 115–32.

53. John Webster, "Principles of Systematic Theology," *International Journal of Systematic Theology* 11 (2009): 56–71, reprinted in Webster, *Domain of the Word*, 133–49.

54. John Webster, "What Makes Theology Theological?," *Journal of Analytic Theology* 3 (2015): 17–28, reprinted in Webster, *God without Measure*, vol. 1, 213–23.

history, and culture must be mapped in expansive form *sub ratione Dei*,[55] as "ordered by and toward God in Christ by the Spirit's power."[56] Doctrinal emphases deserved to be distributed accordingly.[57]

The treatment offered in *The Culture of Theology* was in no sense final. As we read the text today, it is obvious that vastly more has since been said about many of the themes, and Webster himself would not have wished us to regard the work as representative of his mature thought. Although he did occasionally reference the material, he did not reissue it as a whole. Much of his later writing was itself seen only as preparatory to a projected five- (initially three-) volume *Systematic Theology*, which would relativize all of it. In his later years, Webster would have wanted us to hear much more about God, creation, and history, and about how theology's location is not so much the location of the gospel *simpliciter*, or at any rate of the gospel as portrayed *only* in the idiom deployed in the Burns Lectures, but of the gospel of the entire outworking of the Triune God's free and loving resolve to have fellowship with creatures. The contrast that matters, he would have suggested, is not merely between a theology that treats the culture of the gospel or the church as primary and a theology in which the investments of intellectual history (and of one phase of it in particular) have come to assume that status. Insofar as "contrast" is the right approach, what is required is a contrast between a theology that starts and ends with the perfect God who creates and saves and a theology that—perversely—does not. As the

55. Thomas Aquinas, *Summa Theologiae* 1a 1, 7.

56. Webster, *Domain of the Word*, 7.

57. For some examples of what it might mean to configure core doctrines in due order and proportion, see John Webster, "*Rector et iudex super omnia genera doctrinarum?* The Place of the Doctrine of Justification," in *What Is Justification About? Reformed Contributions to an Ecumenical Theme*, ed. Michael Weinrich and John P. Burgess (Grand Rapids: Eerdmans, 2009), 35–56, reprinted in Webster, *God without Measure*, vol. 1, 159–75; John Webster, "'It Was the Will of the Lord to Bruise Him': Soteriology and the Doctrine of God," in *God of Salvation: Soteriology in Theological Perspective*, ed. Ivor J. Davidson and Murray A. Rae (Burlington, VT: Ashgate, 2011), 15–34, reprinted in revised form in Webster, *God without Measure*, vol. 1, 143–57; John Webster, "The Place of Christology in Systematic Theology," in *The Oxford Handbook of Christology*, ed. Francesca Aran Murphy (Oxford: Oxford University Press, 2015), 611–27, reprinted as "Christology, Theology, Economy: The Place of Christology in Systematic Theology," in Webster, *God without Measure*, vol. 1, 43–58.

lectures had begun to indicate, the deficiencies of modern theologians are illustrative only of the tendency to consider the wrong sort of history as normative. Ultimately, making that point well might for Webster have meant saying less about theology as a "culture" at all (or about "conversations" or "public covenants") and at the same time saying a good deal more about the relationship between theology's intellectual and moral responsibilities and other forms of creaturely being and action within the purposes of God.

A great many of these developments are, I think, already firmly underway in the Burns Lectures, in their prevailing insistence that it is God's wondrous work with us, not our human temporal situation, that is central for any definition of theological work. What is significant is that the later Webster would, I believe, have wished to secure a stronger account of human history and creaturely life in general by depicting the biblical economy of salvation as the wondrous movement in which we discover how vast and sheerly generous is God's self-communicative relationship to creation and creatures in the first place. Saying less about social anthropology or philosophy would mean no narrowing of the intellectual or historical focus, but quite the reverse; theology's endeavors could be stated all the more positively because of it. Thus might be illustrated Webster's contention: a seriously theological theology actually has more, not less, to offer when it comes to engaging those who stand outside its confession.

The reference-points would have differed. Thomas would undoubtedly have featured strongly; Reformed Orthodoxy would have been handled more positively; Calvin would have remained a great hero, though perhaps not quite—after all—the last great Protestant theologian of the Spirit (cf. 89). The Bible would have been the Triune God's communication with rational creatures rather than "the primary bearer of Christian culture" (cf. 65); more would have been said of its properties and of the Spirit's illumination of created intelligence in its reception; divine formation of theologians by the text as much as the rhetorical duties of theologians before the text might have been a favored theme. The ascetic dimensions of theology would likely have been explored in subtler terms, with reference to patristic and medieval texts; the recurring emphasis on "devastation" would have been scaled back a little; there might well have been a large amount more on the theologian's work as joyful contemplation, and on the ways in which the intellectual acts of theology relate to other applications of the mind.

As it stands, *The Culture of Theology* has received very little by way of explicit critical interaction. Some of the criticisms directed toward Webster's theology in general might doubtless be applied to his case in this text. For some, his doctrine of the church, and by extension his account of theology itself, remains distinctly idealized, for all its qualifications. It is a blueprint, it is said: indifferent to, dismissive of the vital work that still has to be done by empirical engagement—historical, social-scientific, practical-theological—and by the concrete disciplines of ethics and missiology. According to critiques of this kind, Webster's enduring concern that ecclesiology must be distinguished from mere ethnography is surely unnecessary, misleading even. The people of God are a society of creatures in time and space—summoned, sustained, and purposed by divine action, yes, but also called to exist in an actual history of knowing, hearing, following, and attesting in the world. On that reading, the dynamics of human as well as divine action and the complex processes by which theological activity in all its forms might be said to be shaped and led by the Spirit amid the political, social, and moral density of creaturely existence do require to be specified; otherwise, the doctrine of God swamps everything in a way that Scripture itself does not suggest, and creation, providence, anthropology, morals, and ministry are not set forth in their due proportions.

The kind of theology sketched in the Burns Lectures might be alleged to illustrate some of these problems. Does it not offer only indirect or implicit thoughts on what a theological curriculum shaped by the favored principles might look like, or how it might in practice manage to operate in a university context, or what the roles of theological work might be in regard to public discourse in a postmodern world? Does not the account of Christian virtue, lovely as it is, remain quite stylized? Does not the commendation of awed textual reading emerge at the last in fairly general terms, even lacking in the very exegesis it celebrates? Did not canon, tradition, and dogma take form amid vastly messier circumstances than Webster's handling concedes, and does this not obligate less ambitious claims about their functional status? And if we look back upon Webster's exposition of theology's embodied setting as the church, is not "church" today a much more fragmented, marginal, and contested reality than ever? Do not the further cultural shifts of the past two decades render the questions concerning a supposedly unitary culture of faith across history's fractured story all the more acute? If the place of church and theology in all manner of settings locally and globally has continued to change far more rapidly and profoundly than many in Oxford or Dunedin in 1998 might have guessed, what else might an account of the discipline need now to say regarding its identity and tasks in today's world?

Webster himself was well aware of these general concerns and ventured various sorts of responses to a number of them. As all who interacted with him personally found, he remained modest and gracious in his approach: tenacious in some commitments, certainly, but open to persuasion in others and ready to modulate emphases in an enduring quest to say things better; this attitude, for him, was an important aspect of systematic theology's obligation to keep on reading Scripture in the company of the church. Yet he would likely have considered the critical themes, thus stated at least, quite naive, even an evasion of the entire point of his argument in these lectures. Whatever he might have wished to say differently in later years, a fundamental conviction would not have changed: history is vital; everything hinges upon what kind of history one takes to matter most. The lectures are clear that the sociocultural conditions of theologians vary hugely from situation to situation, that in that sense external context is indeed of unavoidable relevance, that theologians are human agents, engaged in fragile works of thought, speech, and action in time and space: contingent, embodied, gendered, finite, fallible. Their particular habitations, they must come to learn, are indeed but little "bits" of a tradition; gospel culture as they know it is ever marked by its own peculiarities and failures (lectures 1 and 6). Gospel culture as such is not, however, coterminous with their experience or their efforts, nor can it be adequately appraised as if it were. Whatever else is to be said, there is a Word, the evangel of the Triune God. "Context" in worldly terms, modern or otherwise, is not the chief (far less only) thing to say about the location of those who hear it: theology exists, first and foremost, in the situation that is brought into being by God's free and exquisitely generous desire that creatures should know him and his self-movement to make that happen; it is subject at every point to the ways, means, and ends of his unfettered perfection in all its saving adequacy.

For the later Webster, it would be essential to say that whatever use ecclesiology may make of ethnography, metaphysical specification remains crucial. Theological speech about the church cannot be reduced to talk of human social nature or action *simpliciter*: the church is a reality established in the mystery set forth in Christ, and thus a society elected, called, gathered, sanctified, and directed by divine movement. The church's social-historical phenomena must indeed be picked out and discussed, but these features can at no point be identified or construed in isolation from God and God's works.[58]

Again, as lecture 6 here at least aspired to demonstrate, practical divinity matters entirely; practical divinity will, however, begin to be addressed and implemented wisely only in light of God's wondrous declaration concerning himself and us. The later Webster would wish to extend and intensify that principle significantly. Christian ethics, he would argue at length, remains a contemplative science in the first instance, for it is concerned with the reality of creaturely moral being as announced by the gospel. Only that reality, the truth that our situation has been primordially established and redemptively reordered by divine goodness, can be basis for right moral knowledge and action. "There is a material order to dogmatic-moral and practical-ethical theology, in which inquiry into nature precedes attention to circumstances."[59]

Webster would not waver from the insistence that faith's practical energy and its outcomes, like its genesis, must be governed all along the line by reflection on what it is that God is about in the reconciliation and perfection of his rational creatures in Christ by the Spirit. In this, he would say, stands no excusal whatever from

58. See in particular John Webster, "'In the Society of God': Some Principles of Ecclesiology," in *Perspectives on Ecclesiology and Ethnography*, ed. Pete Ward (Grand Rapids: Eerdmans, 2012), 200–222, reprinted in Webster, *God without Measure*, vol. 1, 177–94.

59. John Webster, "Introduction: *Agere sequitur esse*," in Webster, *God without Measure*, vol. 2, 1–4, at 3.

creaturely task, only freedom from false perceptions of task.[60] The policy-formation of faith, the discernment of all its real-life obligations, deserves to be pursued in deliverance from self-preoccupation. The later Webster would continue to push back very firmly against a criticism that speech about God and God's action as theology's first obligation must somehow displace human reality: he would wish to say yet more clearly and carefully than he had earlier that just the opposite is the case.

Such ways of projecting Webster's probable responses on the basis of his mature work are, of course, simplistic; his corpus as a whole offers a vastly subtler treatment of the fundamental themes and a continuing effort to nuance matters more carefully. The want of its final synthesis is very great; but what we have is rich indeed and deserves to be read with enduring care, not least for its immense endeavors to underscore the connection between doctrine and practice. The assessment of his work at large, not least its formative forces, remains in its infancy. There have been some evidences of due appreciation, and important ventures of more substantial critical engagement are underway.[61] Other commentary to date has been of mixed quality, particularly where it has expected Webster to answer questions he resolved not to ask, or has misconstrued his doctrine of God or Scripture or church, or (not least) has oversimplified his intellectual development—perhaps implying that he eventually left Barth behind altogether, or became an unreconstructed Thomist, or embarked on some neo-Reformed scholastic path. Theological theology found different kinds of formulations across his career, but amid the undoubted changes, as he himself appraised them, lay some deep continuities and sheer growth in understanding how to put things. Viewed alongside his later writing, the Burns Lectures offer an important glimpse of some of this.

Though Webster's theology here and beyond strongly emphasized ecclesial setting, he continued to operate in university contexts, his

60. For developed reflections along these lines, see John Webster, "'Where Christ Is': Christology and Ethics," in *Christology and Ethics*, ed. F. LeRon Shults and Brent Waters (Grand Rapids: Eerdmans, 2010), 32–55, reprinted in Webster, *God without Measure*, vol. 2, 5–27.

61. See in particular Michael Allen and R. David Nelson, eds., *A Companion to the Theology of John Webster* (Grand Rapids: Eerdmans, forthcoming).

arguments for the most part directed toward academic peers and students. His case, as he recognized, might have taken different forms in seminary or church-college environments. As do all who inhabit them, he continued to find that academic institutions present challenges, and theology ever has its struggles, whatever might be said. Some universities prove more hospitable than others; the brokenness of divinity's practitioners in any context generates its own tragedies. Webster would be deeply esteemed by some, but he did not cease to encounter others who failed to understand the motivations of his work or who were all too obviously discomfited by his abilities in expressing them. For all the continuing evolution in theology's environments, and for all his own considerable contributions to the rehabilitation of dogmatics in the English-speaking world and beyond, he thought the state of the field not so very different years later. There were reasons to be cheerful about some developments, particularly the recovery of conviction, within certain strands of theological work at least, that "in Scripture the breath of the divine Word quickens reason to knowledge and love of God."[62] But the need for retrieval, seen not as romantic conservatism but as "the expectant search for new possibilities,"[63] remained pressing, and constructive dogmatics was as important as ever. Its patience, confidence, and hope were founded upon the promises of God: that was good enough.

As *The Culture of Theology* had begun to show, theology is spiritual privilege and task; its most pressing need, in worldly terms, remains the sanctification of its teachers: God's work, certainly, but an inescapable summons also to human subjects. In his enduring delight in the instruction of Holy Scripture in the purposes of God, in his endless burrowing into the resources of the tradition as living witness, and in his own serious and dogged but also humble, prayerful, and

62. Webster, "Biblical Reasoning," 751.

63. Webster, *Word and Church*, xiii (preface to 2016 edition). For Webster's assessment of the impulse as variously represented in a mode of twentieth-century systematics and his concern also to avoid the *wrong* kinds of valorization of the past, see his "Theologies of Retrieval," in *Oxford Handbook of Systematic Theology*, 583–99. On the need to speak carefully of the relationship between revelation and church, see also John Webster, "*Ressourcement* Theology and Protestantism," in Ressourcement: *A Movement for Renewal in Twentieth-Century Catholic Theology*, ed. Gabriel Flynn and Paul D. Murray (Oxford: Oxford University Press, 2012), 482–94.

joyful pursuit of theology's responsibilities, Webster himself exemplified a great many of the principles he commends in the lectures.

As he wrote in the year before his death, "The concern to interpret theology's cultural setting not in its own terms but in terms derived from the gospel" remains ever "of considerable importance. The human work of theology is a cultural activity, the matter of the gospel is not; even as it announces itself in creaturely forms, the matter of the gospel is God."[64] The vision grew and deepened; it assuredly did not fade. As one expression of its beauty, these lectures remain a remarkable exercise in the gloriously positive and fulfilling as well as intensely demanding matter of which they speak.

---

64. Webster, *Word and Church*, xii (preface to 2016 edition).

1

Culture

The Shape of Theological Practice

CHRISTIAN FAITH, and therefore Christian theology, emerges out of the shock of the gospel. Christian faith, and therefore Christian theology, takes its rise in the comprehensive interruption of all things in Jesus Christ, for he, Jesus Christ, now present in the power of the Holy Spirit, is the great catastrophe of human life and history. In him, all things are faced by the one who absolutely dislocates and no less absolutely reorders. To this regenerate event, this abolition and re-creation, Christian faith, and therefore Christian theology, offers perplexed and delighted testimony. That perplexity and delight—that sense of being at one and the same time overwhelmed and consumed yet remade and reestablished—are at the heart of the church, or as we might call it, Christian culture. Christian culture is the assembly of forms and practices which seeks somehow to inhabit the world which is brought into being by the staggering good news of Jesus Christ, the world of the new creation. "Behold," says the enthroned one in the climactic scene of the Apocalypse, "I make all things new" (Rev. 21:5). Christian theology is an activity in a culture which reaches out toward that miracle, sharing that culture's astonishing new life.

That, in briefest outline, is the heart of what I want to say in these lectures. My proposal is that much can be gained by thinking of Christian theology as part of Christian culture—as one of the practices which make up the disturbing, eschatological world of Christian faith and life. Christian theology flourishes best when it has deep roots in the region, the cultural space, which is constituted by Christian faith and its confession of the gospel. Moreover, within my proposal about the nature and tasks of Christian theology there is a diagnosis of the current state of the discipline. If Christian theology today is sometimes in disarray—as, indeed, I believe it is—then one of the major reasons is its dislocation from its cultural place. What inhibits Christian theology is not only the generally inhospitable intellectual and institutional environment in which it has to flourish but its lack of roots in the traditions of Christian belief and practice which are the soil in which it can grow. It is, in other words, as much internal disorder as external discouragement which cramps the exercise of Christian theology. And if this is so, then one of the most important tasks for Christian theology in the present is its reintegration back into the culture of Christian faith. Yet it is crucial to my argument that that culture is not a steady, stable world which affords those who belong to it the security of being *placed* in some definitive way. It is, paradoxically, a place which is no place, a place made by the presence of God who invades and interrupts all places. Being located in that kind of culture is equally a matter of *dislocation*, of discovering how to be more theological by encountering once again the shock of the gospel.

In using terms like "the culture of Christian faith" and "the culture of theology," I have three things in mind. First, Christian theology, like any other form of reflective activity, takes place in a culture, that is, in a public or social space. Theological ideas both bear and are borne along by cultural practices, and cannot be isolated from the arena in which such practices occur. Discerning the plausibility of theological ideas is not a matter merely of seeing how they work in the abstract but rather of trying to figure out the functions which they perform in the particular world in which they have their home: the strange world of the gospel and the church. A good deal of what I want to say in these lectures concerns the components of Christian culture which bear on the practices of Christian theology—its canonical texts; its corporate, historical, and institutional shape as the ecclesial community; its ways of engaging with other cultural worlds; and its strategies for submitting itself to judgment. One of the things we need to undertake is an exercise in theological ethnography: a theological depiction (rather than a critical inquiry into the possibility) of the world of the church in which theology happens.

Second, I use the word "culture" to suggest that theology needs to be "cultivated." The encouragement of good theology requires that certain interventions be made in order to promote certain practices and achieve certain ends. Thus, for example, I shall argue that among the most important practices which need to be cultivated—especially at the present time—are textual practices, habits of reading. There can be few things more necessary for the renewal of Christian theology than the promotion of awed reading of classical Christian texts, scriptural and other, precisely because a good deal of modern Christian thought has adopted habits of mind which have led to disenchantment with the biblical canon and the traditions of paraphrase and commentary by which the culture of Christian faith has often been sustained. Such practices of reading and interpretation, and the educational and political strategies which surround them, are central to the task of creating the conditions for the nurture of Christian theology.

Third, fostering the practice of Christian theology will involve the cultivation of persons with specific habits of mind and soul. It will involve "culture" in the sense of *formation*. To put the matter in its simplest and yet most challenging form: being a Christian theologian involves the struggle to become a certain kind of person, one shaped by the culture of Christian faith. But once again, this is not some sort of unproblematic, passive socialization into a world of already achieved meanings and roles. It is above all a matter of interrogation by the gospel, out of which the theologian seeks to make his or her own certain dispositions and habits, filling them out in disciplined speech and action. Such seeking is painful; as a form of conversion it involves the strange mixture of resistance and love which is near the heart of real dealings with the God who slays us in order to make us alive. Good theological practice depends on good theologians; and good theologians are—among other things—those formed by graces which are the troubling, eschatological gifts of the Holy Spirit.

Before proceeding any further with making my proposal, however, two introductory comments need to be made if we are not to get off track. The first is a qualification about my title: the culture of theology. For all its usefulness when deployed to talk of Christian theology in relation to Christian faith, the term "culture" has some definite limitations. Certainly, Christian faith is a culture: like any other distinctive, large-scale pattern of human life, it is a historically embodied project through which the world is given meaning. And I hope to show that we may learn a good deal more about the nature and tasks of Christian theology by considering it in relation to that historical project than we do by subsuming theology under some ideal of disengaged, acultural critical reason. Yet the notion of culture begins to reach the limits of its applicability when we realize that, for its practitioners, Christian faith is not simply a human project, a set of human undertakings and activities. Christian faith is eschatological. It is a response to God's devastation of human life and history by the miracle of grace. Moreover, the response which we make is itself somehow contained within the miracle. Christian faith and culture are never simply a matter of appropriating that miracle, making it "our own," for grace is always utterly free and present only as the event of gift. If all that is so, then there is a necessary tension—even, in one sense, an antithesis—between "faith" and "culture." For all that it may be necessary to speak of the culture of Christian faith, Christian culture is in one real sense an impossibility: How can the shock of the gospel become a culture without being stripped of its sheer difference and otherness? At the very least, we have to say that the culture of Christian faith and therefore the culture of theology stand beneath the sign of their contradiction, which is the gospel of God.

The second introductory comment is an anticipation of dissent on the part of you, the audience. I have no doubt that to some of you what I have to say will seem to fly in the face of some of the prevailing trends of modern theology. That's because it does. My diagnosis of the present state of the discipline, as well as the therapy which I have to offer, cuts across the grain of what—despite some pretty heavy shelling—remain well-entrenched intellectual conventions in post-Enlightenment Christianity. Nor will what I have to say be particularly congenial to those whose turn from the Enlightenment has led them into one or other variety of postmodernism; however chastened by the genealogists, I remain unrepentantly (though not, I hope, belligerently) committed to grand narratives and substance ontology, which are in my judgment far more serviceable to anyone seeking to give an account of the Christian gospel than are philosophies of playful contingency. But I fear that the expression of such commitments may raise all sorts of anxieties. Do they not inevitably lead to the ecclesiastical captivity of theology, its withdrawal from both modernity and postmodernity into a closed (premodern?) religious world, its isolation from interchange and conversation, which are the essential conditions for intellectual life? And does it not mean the prosecution of a style of theology which, devoid of criticism, slips into becoming repetitious, self-perpetuating, and, in the end, ideological? These are, indeed, crucial questions and will occupy us much over the course of these lectures. At this stage, let me merely indicate the way I hope to respond to them. I will try to argue that the capacity of Christian theology to sustain lively conversations with what lies outside its culture, as well as to engage in serious self-criticism, is dependent upon its grasp of its own proper object: the gift of the presence of God in Jesus Christ through the power of the Holy Spirit. Because that object is what (who) it is—the living God among us with sheerly intrusive force—the culture of Christian faith and theology is at the same time an anti-culture. It is the site of a struggle against the domestic idolatry of Christendom, against the creation and establishment and defense of settled representations of God. And if this is so, then the cultivation of Christian culture, far from isolating theology from subversion through critique, is in fact the essential precondition for a theological practice characterized above all by repentance.

⫸⬥⫷

First, then, we tackle the question: to what extent may we think of Christianity as a culture and of Christian theology as a practice within a culture?

What is a *culture*? In using the term I am not referring to "high culture"; nor am I using it in quite the same sense that Richard Niebuhr
famously used it in *Christ and Culture* to refer to the world which lies
outside church and faith. Rather, at risk of a dramatic oversimplifica-
tion of the issues, I mean something like this: a culture is a space or
region made up of human activities. It is a set of intentional patterns
of human action which have sufficient coherence, scope, and duration to constitute a way of life. A culture is not occasional (limited
to a single fragment of time) or utterly local (restricted to a mere
handful of persons in a particular place), for it must have sufficient
range and comprehensiveness to make a world within which primary,
enduring aspects of human life and experience can be negotiated. The
elements of a culture—language, ideas and beliefs, shared patterns
of behavior, roles, dispositions and habits, norms of evaluation, and
instruments of identity—assemble together to form an arena within
which thought, speech, and action are meaningful, and human life
can be projected. Thus defined, culture is the frame of actions; it is
the larger field within which human life-acts take place, and without
which they would lack purpose and intelligibility. Our capacity to
formulate ends for ourselves, to undertake actions to realize such
ends, and to evaluate our performance—all are dependent upon a
sense of orientation in historical and social space. Culture is thus
what Heidegger called the "region of objects"[1] or what the phe-
nomenologist Alfred Schutz called a "finite province of meaning." If
these geographic, spatial metaphors point to the way in which culture
locates human life and activity, we need also to bear in mind that
culture is also history, giving order and direction to discrete temporal
activities, and enabling us to see human life as a coherent project
through time. In sum: culture is that through which human life and
activities have enduring shape, identity, and meaning.

What of the term "practice"? Once again, at the risk of oversim-
plification or caricature, we might say something like this: A practice

1. Martin Heidegger, "Phenomenology and Theology," in *The Piety of Thinking:
Essays by Martin Heidegger*, ed. James G. Hart and John C. Maraldo (Bloomington:
Indiana University Press, 1976), 5–21, at 6. See also Alfred Schutz, "On Multiple
Realities," in *The Collected Papers of Alfred Schutz*, vol. 1 (The Hague: Nijhoff,
1962), 207–59.

is a set of activities through which human beings pursue complex, socially established goals. Because they are socially established, practices transcend particular practitioners. Undertaking a practice involves playing a role, that is, shaping one's actions in accordance with certain conventions about how to realize the goals that are pursued. And as "conventional" behavior, practices involve us in attending to norms through which we are able to judge whether we have attained our goals, and with what degree of excellence. Culture and practice are clearly mutually defining concepts: part of what constitutes a culture is sets of practices; practices as forms of social activity take place and have their meaning in a cultural region. Thus it is through practices that we inhabit cultural space, as it were colonizing the world, making it habitable as a place in which we may be human.

So far, perhaps, so good. But now we have to ask: How does this affect the way in which think about the tasks of Christian theology?

Intellectual activity is a practice in a culture. Far from being abstract, ahistorical, and asocial, intellectual activity is a complex form of human action which occurs in a determinate cultural locale and, in some measure, takes its shape from that locale's conventions. Intellectual activity is not simply "the life of the mind," if by "mind" we mean some special region *within* me, or perhaps some clear, uncluttered space above and beyond time, society, and persons. "The life of the mind" is not bodiless interiority nor does it consist of a capacity to abstract ourselves from our historical entanglements and look down on them from some privileged vantage point. "The life of the mind" is always the life of the mind *here*, in *this* space. The theological ramifications of this point can best be appreciated by drawing a rather rough-and-ready contrast.

The Enlightenment ideal of absolute reflection has sustained serious damage: from hermeneutical philosophy, from critical theorists, and, most recently, from the clutch of thinkers we call postmodernists. Yet many of the reigning models of intellectual practice (and especially some to which we appeal in pursuing the theological disciplines) remain wedded to the idea that it is the task of intellectual reflection to stand apart from all determinate states of affairs and all cultural locales so that we can think critically about them. The aim of the life of the intellect is to reach judgments about the conditions of possibility of any particular cultural configuration. This act of judgment is transcendent, taking place in a kind of absolute space. Rational activity is by definition activity which operates according to universal, context-invariant criteria which draw the world into the presence of the inquiring mind and make it an object for inspection and critique. Such a model of the life of the mind tends to be pre-occupied with the question of how we can disabuse ourselves of false notions, mere derivative and unverified opinion. This is particularly the case in the original sponsors of the ideal—Descartes and, above all, Locke—for whom epistemology provided the only way of break-ing the logjam of appeal to authoritative cultural representations in religion and morals. But the same fundamental motivation often animated its application in theology, for example, to questions of the history and interpretation of the biblical texts. What is important to notice here is that the critical task performed by epistemology tends to go hand in hand with a privileging of subjectivity, which in turn reinforces a certain anthropology or picture of the self. That picture, dominated by an ideal of total reflection, stripped the thinker of all particular characteristics derived from history and cultural location and conviction. Thinking is a process of reaching judgments which is undertaken by no one in particular nowhere in particular.

By way of contrast, we may consider an understanding of intel-lectual activity not simply as a mental act but as a practice, not as a mode of consciousness but as a complex operation in a historical, tradition-constituted space. Intellectual activity is, in other words, *regional*. The difference here is that this second account of intellectual activity is not tied to an anthropology in which the constitutive mo-ment is reason's deliverance of the self from the errors of unexamined tradition. On this account of things, mapping the intellectual life will involve us, therefore, in developing something more historical and social in orientation, a sort of ecology of intellectual practices and their habitats. And such an account will not be preoccupied with so-called perennial problems but concerned much more with giving an analytical depiction of what "we" (the inhabitants of this bit of cultural territory) do.

There are some immediate advantages for the pursuit of Chris-tian theology if we think of the intellectual life in such terms. Most obviously, it gives us purchase against the ideals of disengaged reason, interiority, and critique which have exercised such a prevailing influence over our understanding of what learning is and which remain deeply entrenched in the politics and institutions of reflection. Such an understanding of learning and its public forums has rarely been willing to sponsor theological inquiry informed by Christian faith. The realization that that understanding is not absolute but simply a potent and highly successful cultural convention ought to offer considerable relief to the often anxious intellectual conscience of modern theology. And there are other advantages, too. Understanding intellectual life as "regional" (a practice in a particular cultural space) will mean that the particularity of Christian theology will be allowed to be itself without being too anxious about its standing vis-à-vis other disciplines, especially its near neighbors in history and philosophy. And this, in turn, may ease one of the most damaging side effects of modern ideals of critical inquiry, namely their homogenizing tendency, their eliding of difference, and their preference for what is common across all contexts and situations. Or again, calling into question some modern ideals of responsible intellectual activity may help us to begin work on a task which has so far scarcely been touched, namely telling the story of modern theology from the perspective of the culture of faith. Told from that vantage point, the story will not be organized around the idea of gradual release from the tutelage of authority into the free and open spaces of critical inquiry; rather, it will be a story of loss of roots, of detachment, and of the declining accessibility of the space within which to cultivate the Christian life of the mind.

⇒•⇐

To sum up so far: because the notions of culture and practice help us to re-regionalize intellectual activity, integrating reflection back into the historical processes of society, they may prove useful in moving us beyond the bifurcation of Christian theology and the life of Christian communities. Yet it is at just this point that we have to turn the argument back on itself and face a critical theological objection: How can we talk of Christian faith as culture without collapsing into immanence? Does not talk of Christianity as a culture and of theology as a practice in such a culture threaten to erode, suppress, or even supplant talk of God's presence and action? Once Christianity is conceived of as a moral, social, or religious "world," does it not become increasingly difficult to know what critical difference is made by direct talk about God, Christ, Spirit, and so forth? Is not such language easily reduced to becoming symbolic of nothing more than a somewhat anonymous and opaque origin of cultural forms and activities? And when this happens, have we not repeated the unhappy exchange of subjects which so deeply grieved Barth as he surveyed the splendors of nineteenth-century Protestantism?

Along with Kierkegaard, Barth is a crucial witness here. More than any other theological writer of the twentieth century, he urged with a single-minded passion that, for much of the history of modern Protestant theology, talk of God and talk of the cultural realities of the Christian religion have been inversely proportional. The steady expansion of "immanent" accounts of Christianity is matched by the contraction of talk of divine action. And so in what is surely one of the most remarkable pieces of theological prophecy this century, Barth's famous 1919 Tambach Lecture, "The Christian's Place in Society," he urged that the synthesis of Christianity and cultural action which had so dominated the social ethics of the Ritschlian school of theology rested on an entirely inadequate foundation, namely the reduction of the divine to a mere aspect or function of the world of human moral and cultural endeavor. Barth's dismay about this theology turned upon his deep sense of its fundamental incompatibility with the content of the Christian gospel, above all because it threatened to convert the purely miraculous, unassimilable, and free action of God into some perceptible cultural form with which human activity could then be coordinated. Christ, Barth told his bewildered audience in 1919, is not a cultural principle or mere incitement to moral action; he is "the absolutely *new from above*,"[2] and the life which he imparts is "not our best understanding and experience of God, not our best godliness, not an experience apart from others"; rather, "this new life is that from the third dimension . . . ; it is the world of God breaking through from its self-contained holiness and

2. Karl Barth, "The Christian's Place in Society," in *The Word of God and the Word of Man* (London: Hodder & Stoughton, 1928), 272–327, at 286.

appearing in secular life; it is the bodily resurrection of Christ from the dead."[3] Or as he puts it in a crucial phrase: "Beyond, *trans*: *that* is the crux of the situation; *that* is the source of our life."[4] Yet for Barth, none of this ought to lead us to conclude that Christian faith and culture or society exist in a pure and irreconcilable disjunction or that the gospel cannot somehow assume cultural forms. It is a matter not of denying that Christian faith is a form of life but of seeing that the form of life which Christian faith is both emerges from and is ceaselessly called into question by the resurrection of Jesus from the dead. "The *resurrection* of Jesus Christ from the dead is the power which moves both the world and us, *because* it is the appearance in our corporeality of a *totaliter aliter* constituted corporeality."[5]

There is a quite crucial lesson to be learned here, which is this: the culture of Christian faith is an "eschatological" culture. That is to say, it is a culture which is generated, sustained, and perfected, and also exposed to radical questioning, by the utterly gratuitous presence of God in the risen Jesus through the Holy Spirit's working. By speaking of Christian culture as "eschatological," I am referring to much more than simply the fact that Christian belief includes reference to such themes as Christ's *parousia*, the last judgment and vindication of the elect, or life everlasting. Rather, "eschatological" refers to that single, perfect reality which is the basis and end of all realities, that absolute which, as the origin of all that is, is pure, free, ungraspable, approachable only by virtue of its own prior approach to us in a kind of loving devastation. For Christian faith, that "absolute" is nothing other than God's great "I am," declared in the covenant and uttered supremely in the resurrection of Jesus from the dead: "I am the first and the last, and the living one; I died, and behold, I am alive for evermore" (Rev. 1:17–18). He, the risen Jesus, the new (counter-) creation, *is* the presence of the eschaton, and it is because of him that Christian culture is eschatological. Brought into being by his disruptive presence and thereby pointed toward its proper end, the world of Christian faith is the strange cultural space in which the re-creative work of God is confessed. How can this exotic culture be depicted?

3. Barth, "Christian's Place in Society," 286–87.
4. Barth, "Christian's Place in Society," 321.
5. Barth, "Christian's Place in Society," 323.

Its origin lies in the divine call from all eternity, which is identical with the self-declaration and summons of the risen Christ: "I am with you always" (Matt. 28:20). Christian culture exists as the fruit of that divine self-manifestation which, in its imperative force, appoints humanity to fellowship with God and commissions humanity to life ordered toward that fellowship. As an appointment rooted solely in the divine will, the summons of the risen Christ entirely transcends human worth, expectation, or capacity; indeed, it is a summons only because over and above this it is a divine making, a determination of us for life in fellowship with God. Such a divine "making" is simply not communicable; there is no point at which God's action retires in favor of human undertakings. And so Christian eschatological culture is never just "made" by us in any straightforward sense. In one sense, of course, it *is* made by us: to say anything less would be docetic. But our making of a culture is as it were our inhabiting of a space in which we have been set, acting out roles and fulfilling tasks to which we have been appointed, and doing so with an energy which is God's own gift. It is this, of course, which sets Christianity at a distance from both the ethics of culture in bourgeois religion and the aesthetics or poetics of culture in some varieties of postmodernism; neither can make much sense of cultural forms as *generated*.

Christian culture thus originates in the divine summons; this is Christian difference seen in terms of cultural archaeology. The goal or end of Christian culture is Christian difference as teleology. The *telos* of Christian culture is the lordly rule of Jesus Christ in all things. Christian culture stretches out beyond itself to a future which is the manifestation of God's glory, the utter radiance of God, who is all in all. The perfection of Christian culture is thus not some immanent teleology, a matter of self-realization through historical process, and working toward that perfection is a matter of struggling to make the forms of culture transparent to a future which is God's. Christian culture has a distinct and different sense of its own history: existing from the divine call, it exists toward the divine consummation in the coming of Jesus Christ.

Third, emerging from this origin in the resurrection of Jesus as the divine summons, and having its end in the final manifestation of his consummate lordly rule over all things, Christian eschatological culture is a place where God's overthrow of sin attains a special visibility. Doubly determined by its origin and end, it is a place where convertedness can be discerned. Christian culture is the place where human life is caught up into the process of what the old Protestant dogmaticians called "continual" or "second" conversion, in which the effectiveness of regeneration is brought to bear on human ruin. Continual conversion is the sanctification of human life through its mortification and vivification in Christ. Christian culture, caught up in Christ's sanctifying work, is thus characterized by a pattern of *overthrow and reestablishment*. Being in this culture means simultaneously being put to death and made alive. This pattern, of course, is nothing other than the baptismal pattern of dying and rising with Christ, which forms the deep structure of life in Christ, both as its divine genesis and as its distinctive moral and spiritual shape. The discriminating mark of Christian culture, poised between this origin and this end, is thus, baptism. For Christian culture is that space, that set of human forms, which owes its origin to and derives its particular configuration from the paschal mystery of Christ, presented to the believer in the common life of the church through the work of the Holy Spirit.

What are the implications for the practice of Christian theology if it takes place in this particular space in the world? To put the matter at its simplest: it means that Christian theological reflection is poised uneasily between location and dislocation. To make the point, we may reflect on a passage of early Christian exhortation:

> You have not come to what may be touched, a blazing fire, and darkness, and gloom, and a tempest, and the sound of a trumpet, and a voice whose words made the hearers entreat that no further messages be spoken to them. For they could not endure the order that was given, "If even a beast touches the mountain, it shall be stoned." Indeed, so terrifying was the sight that Moses said, "I tremble with fear." But you have come to Mount Zion and to the city of the living God, the heavenly Jerusalem, and to innumerable angels in festal gathering, and to the assembly of the first-born who are enrolled in heaven, and to a judge who is God of all, and to the spirits of the righteous made perfect, and to Jesus, the mediator of a new covenant, and to the sprinkled blood that speaks more graciously than the blood of Abel. (Heb. 12:18–24)

This remarkable passage can be read as a depiction of the spiritual space within which one early Christian community found itself. It is a space characterized by a dialectic of homelessness and belonging. Like much in Hebrews, the passage revolves around a contrast between what is tangible and what is "heavenly." "You have not come to what may be touched": that is, the spiritual space of the people of Jesus is not the district around some palpable, local theophany. Fire, darkness, gloom and tempest, the sound of the trumpet, and the terrifying voice—all the appurtenances of Sinai—are too dense, too tactile. While there are, of course, "Platonic" overtones here, the real point of the imagery is to say: the true space of the people of Jesus is *other*. Yet the description which is offered of this true space is nevertheless cast in densely *cultural* imagery: a mountain, the foundation of the new order; a heavenly city; an assembly. It is place, structure, and society, but place, structure, and society transformed beyond mere tangible locality by the fact that at its center is the living God, the judge, Jesus himself. The Christian community lives, acts, and suffers in *this* space—a space constituted by the personal rule and authoritative speech of Jesus. Only this space is unshakeable, the Letter to the Hebrews continues, for only this space is a "kingdom," established by the God who shakes not only earth but heaven.

The space of Christian theology is this space. Its identity, its tasks, and its modes of operation are shaped by its occupation of this particular space. Its choices about what constitutes its significant questions, and about how those questions are to be pursued, are determined by its inhabitation of this city and its keeping company with angels and the assembly of the firstborn. However bizarre this may seem as a description of intellectual activity, I do not think anything less can be said about Christian theology without a fundamental mis-mapping. Yet, because it exists *here*, theology must be pervaded by a sense that it has "not come to what may be touched." What we are indicating when we point out the region of faith and theology is thus not simply a set of determinate practices, a configuration of human life which can finally be represented. Rather, we are indicating a process of sanctification, a divine undertaking, a heavenly reality of which there can no more be an ethnography than there can be a psychology or an economics or an aesthetics. Nor, in one important sense, can there even be a theology of this space. However much we may stress that theology is properly located *here*, it is always, if it really makes a reference to its proper object, faced by its own refutation of itself.

If we look at this dialectical picture of the situation of Christian theology in a little more detail, we note, first, that Christian theology is an activity in this space and is therefore characterized by a certain regional specificity. Christian theology is not a free but a positive science, and its *positum*, the given which determines its nature and tasks, is the eschatological culture of Christian faith. Christian theology thus has a particular identity, an identity which, moreover, is not merely a human religious or intellectual construction but something which in a real sense is given and *required*. One very important implication here is that the Christian theologian also has a specific identity: as an inhabitant of this eschatological space, he or she is a "practitioner within the Christian tradition."[6] Once again, the full force of this claim can be felt only by setting it in contrast to some commanding modern notions of intellectual activity. As the bearer of a particular identity, as one caught up within the process of overthrowing and reestablishment, which is potently signified to us in baptism, the Christian theologian is called to break free from an influential modern understanding of human identity, according to which the shape of my life is nothing other than the externalization of my freedom or the expression of that freedom in the assumption of contingent commitments. In intellectual form, that modern account of human identity surfaces in the assumption that intellectual dignity resides in freedom of inquiry, and that freedom of inquiry is undetermination by situation—all of which is a transposition into the life of the mind of political and spiritual ideals, with which Christian theology has no little quarrel. Taking a different direction here will mean a reevaluation of the kinds of competencies which are thought indispensable for undertaking the task of Christian theology. At the very least, it will mean that competence in the rules of life of some strand of the Christian tradition will have much higher profile in assessing theological work than it customarily enjoys in much modern theology. Attentive, adaptable familiarity with what goes on in the strange space of Christian faith, prayer, and work, as

6. George Schner, *Education for Ministry: Reform and Renewal in Theological Education* (Kansas City, MO: Sheed & Ward, 1993), xiii.

well as a mature inhabitation of the roles which are fitting in that space, are not—as is so often suggested—a *hindrance* to thought, but rather thought's social and historical anchor. The conditions for theology's success include crucial internal conditions.

But if theology is thus in one sense "fixed," the one upon whom it is fixed—the living God at the heart of the new Jerusalem, the judge—is always a source of overwhelming and destabilizing. Over against some postmodernism, this does not mean that "givenness" is always mere idolatry, or that theology has to stand apart from any ideologically constituted space. For the Letter to the Hebrews, we may remind ourselves, we really have come to Mount Zion and the city of the living God. But because it is *this* city, *this* space to which we have come, then alongside the permanent task of focusing the identity of Christian theology there has to be another task, which Barth once called "a penultimate 'deassuring' of theology, or . . . a theological warning against theology."[7] He went on to describe this as "a warning against the idea that [theology's] propositions or principles are certain in themselves." Perhaps we may put it thus: the God whose presence and activity generate the eschatological culture which is Christian theology's space is mystery. God as mystery means, not God unknown, but God in the utter freedom with which he makes himself present to us. God cannot be objectified, that is, rendered as a feature in some assemblage of cultural forms, even (especially!) the forms of Christian eschatological culture. "We cannot," Barth noted, "give the Word of God its own sphere in the world which is known to us and which is to be conceptually classified by us. All our delimitations can only seek to be signals or alarms to draw attention to the fact that God's Word is and remains God's, not bound and not to be attached to this thesis or to that antithesis."[8] However crucial it may be that theology be tied to its object and grasped as a positive science operative in a particular sphere, it is equally crucial that the object of theology is *subject*. The living God is not a passive and silent natural object, nor an item of cultural capital; rather, this God is eloquent, disturbing, spiritual presence, a consuming fire more dangerous even than that tangible fire of Sinai.

7. Karl Barth, *Church Dogmatics* I/1 (Edinburgh: T&T Clark, 1975), 164–65.
8. Barth, *Church Dogmatics* I/1, 164.

My suggestion, then, is that the peculiar character of the Christian confession of the gospel, and its sense of itself as what goes on in its region, are such that Christian theology stands in a complex relation to its culture, both located and dislocated by the reality which brings it into being. Theological activity characteristically displays a tendency to give profile to one or the other pole of the dialectic, to function, that is, in what Jonathan Smith calls either a "locative" or a "utopian" fashion.[9] The prominence accorded to one particular strategy will depend by and large upon the judgments reached by theologians about the current health and needs of Christian culture, about the context in which faith and theology find themselves, and about what plans of action need to be followed if it is to fulfill its vocation of indicating the gospel of Jesus Christ. The theologian will thus not only be a skilled inhabitant of a particular cultural world but will demonstrate skills in reaching judgments about circumstance, and skills in reading his or her situation well. In some situations, it may be that Christian culture is considered to be in danger of becoming "de-regionalized," that is, prone to cut itself adrift from that through which it acquires its specific identity, perhaps because of the weight of authority accorded to factors external to the region of Christian faith. When this is the case, then Christian theology may adopt a strategy of emphasizing the need to safeguard specificity. In doing so, theology will normally give profile to those aspects of Christian faith and practice which heighten difference, dissonance, and boundaries. My own judgment, for what it's worth, is that for all the dangers associated with this strategy—closure, mislocation of boundaries, indifference to the task of self-critique—it is one which in the current situation ought most to command our attention. In other situations, it may be that Christian culture is threatened with idolatry—with what Richard Niebuhr identified as "henotheism," that is, "the social faith whose god (value-center and cause) is society itself."[10] If that is so, then Christian theology may feel required to adopt a tactic which will heighten the sheerly other, uncapturable

9. Jonathan Z. Smith, *Map Is Not Territory: Studies in the History of Religion* (Leiden: Brill, 1978).

10. H. Richard Niebuhr, *Radical Monotheism and Western Culture* (New York: Harper, 1960), 26–27.

character of that to which Christian culture is a response. But in the end the strategies are, in fact, inseparable; what enables theological critique of idolatry is precisely a deeply formed sense of the content of the Christian gospel, and the formation of such a sense cannot bypass the social processes of coming to learn how to understand and act out Christian difference.

Let me try to draw together the threads of the argument by suggesting that the practice of Christian theology in the culture of Christian faith requires two things: roots and astonishment. The need for roots was articulated with her unique combination of political astuteness and moral and spiritual compassion by Simone Weil in her book of that title, written in 1943 over the last few months of her life. She wrote,

> To be rooted is perhaps the most important and the least recognized need of the human soul. A human being has roots by virtue of his real, active and natural participation in the life of a community which preserves in living shape certain particular treasures of the past and certain particular expectations for the future. . . . Every human being needs to have multiple roots. It is necessary for him to draw wellnigh the whole of his moral, intellectual and spiritual life by way of the environment of which he forms a natural part.[11]

Though not only a natural community, Christian culture will be worth very little if it does not enable us to order the soul, educating and nourishing us with the discipline of location. And likewise, Christian theology will be not much more than a trivial pursuit if it does not seek to put its roots deep into the troublesome, contrary world of the Christian gospel. In the lectures which follow, I want to explore some of the things which are involved in this discipline of location—reading these texts, exploring these traditions, struggling to be shaped by these habits.

But alongside the need for roots is the no less important need for astonishment. Barth once wrote that "only if there is . . . astonishment

11. Simone Weil, *The Need for Roots: Prelude to a Declaration of Duties towards Mankind* (London: Routledge & Kegan Paul, 1952), 41. See Eric O. Springsted, "Rootedness: Culture and Value," in *Simone Weil's Philosophy of Culture: Readings toward a Divine Humanity*, ed. Richard H. Bell (Cambridge: Cambridge University Press, 1993), 161–88.

. . . can there be serious, fruitful and edifying Christian thought and
utterance."[12] Christian astonishment is the amazed realization that all
human life and thought is undertaken in the presence of Easter, for
Jesus the living one makes himself into our contemporary, startling us
with the fact that he simply *is*. If Christian culture is a strange reality, it is because it seeks to live out that amazement; and if Christian
theology is indeed to be "serious, fruitful and edifying," if it is truly
to live up to the little qualifier "Christian," it cannot be a stranger
to the disruption which amazement brings.

12. Karl Barth, *Church Dogmatics* IV/3 (Edinburgh: T&T Clark, 1961), 287.

2

Texts

Scripture, Reading, and the Rhetoric of Theology

IN THE FIRST LECTURE, I tried to sketch an account of Christian theology as a practice in the eschatological culture of Christian faith. Christian culture is eschatological in the sense that it is a set of astonished human responses to the gospel of the new world. The gospel announces the unheard-of truth that sin and death have been set aside, that human life is caught up in the new creation, and that all are summoned to a life corresponding to the new thing which God has done. Because the passage from death to life which the gospel declares is *absolute*—for it is not just an adjustment of our history but its entire remaking—Christian culture is about the presence of that which is bewilderingly new. Theology, I suggested, has its sphere of operation in this cultural space: in the space of regeneration, convertedness, baptism. Thereby, theology is both *located* and *dislocated*. It is a local activity because it is a practice in the particular human region which the gospel establishes for itself. Yet it is dislocated because the gospel of God can never be commodified, turned into a consumable item in an economy of cultural objects. Theology is a positive science, but its "given" is the unmanageable gift of God's coming in Christ and Spirit.

In this lecture, I want to talk about the place of texts and the reading of texts in that culture of the gospel. In particular, I want to reflect on the relation between theology and Scripture, and most especially on the ways in which the rhetoric of theology ought to be shaped by that relation. To set us on our way, let's listen to a somewhat surprising voice, namely that great despiser of the cult of words, Francis Bacon. Toward the end of *The Advancement of Learning*, written in 1605, as he is summarizing the main headings of sacred theology, Bacon writes,

> in perusing books of divinity, I find many books of controversies; and many of commonplaces and treaties, a mass of positive divinity, as it is made an art; a number of sermons and lectures, and many prolix commentaries upon the Scriptures, with harmonies and concordances: but that form of writing in divinity which in my judgment is of all others most rich and precious, is positive divinity, collected upon particular texts of Scriptures in brief observations; not dilated into commonplaces, not chasing after controversies, not reduced into method of art; a thing abounding in sermons, which will vanish, but defective in books which will remain.[1]

Bacon is an unlikely witness, because his later works on scientific method show him deeply suspicious of the Christian and humanist literary culture of exegesis.[2] Here, however, Bacon gives almost innocent support to a way of doing theology which is largely lost to us, and which, indeed, was already slipping out of Western Christian theology in Bacon's own time. It is that mode of theology which I want to explore today. The "most rich and precious" theology, I want to suggest, is what Bacon calls "positive divinity," that is, "observations upon texts of Scriptures." One of the main tasks of theology is to exemplify and promote close and delighted reading of Holy Scripture as the *viva vox Dei*, the voice of the risen Jesus to his community. This

---

1. Francis Bacon, *The Advancement of Learning*, ed. G. W. Kitchin (London: Dent, 1915), 218.
2. See here W. P. D. Wightman, *Science in a Renaissance Society* (London: Hutchinson, 1972), 158–74; Anthony Grafton, *Defenders of the Text: The Traditions of Scholarship in an Age of Science* (Cambridge: Harvard University Press, 1991).

job is the rather low-level one of "making observations" on the Bible. Moreover, the absorption in Scripture which this requires is to be a primary determinant of the rhetoric of theology. Its core vocabulary, its favored styles of exposition, its manners of address, its modes of persuasion are all to be largely governed by proximity and subordination to the text of Scripture as the place where the gospel is laid bare.

My suggestion, then, is that the theologian's occupation is primarily exegetical and that the necessary concern with other business is only derivative or by extension. However, the cogency of this suggestion depends upon its being undergirded by two further proposals. The first is that we need to give a theological account of the biblical texts as Holy Scripture—that is, as traditions of language which God annexes for the purpose of speaking the gospel to us. The second is that reading and interpreting these texts is not simply a natural affair but an activity of Spirit-generated faith and therefore, again, a matter for theological depiction. In brief: theology has its controlling center in exegesis of Holy Scripture; Holy Scripture is the Word of God; the Word of God summons us to faithful reading.

Before getting into the details, however, we need to address an immediate question: Why does this kind of proposal more than likely strike us as little short of bizarre? Assuming that it is not simply a completely foolish proposal, two related answers could be given. The first explanation of our sense of the oddity of this proposal is the observation that a good deal of modern church life demonstrates loss of practical confidence in Scripture as the primary bearer of Christian culture.[3] If that is so, then sorting out the relation of theology to Scripture is a subdivision of a larger problem, namely, the need for a compelling rediscovery of the church's proper discursive habits. The proper ordering of theology to Scripture rests in part upon attitudes toward and use of Scripture in the church, whose endurance is bound up with its capacity to live out its biblical constitution. "Sacred persistence," says Jonathan Smith, "is primarily exegesis."[4]

3. For just one of many recent arguments along these lines, see Luke Timothy Johnson, "Imagining the World Scripture Imagines," *Modern Theology* 14 (1998): 165–80.

4. Jonathan Z. Smith, "Sacred Persistence: Toward a Redescription of Canon," in *Imagining Religion: From Babylon to Jonestown* (Chicago: University of Chicago Press, 1982), 44.

Ironically, confidence in the capacity of Scripture to serve as carrier for the church's life and mission is in many respects undermined by those institutions most committed to its furtherance: established biblical and theological scholarship and patterns of decision-making in the church which are reluctant to consult the Christian world of meaning first.

Recovery of confidence in that world of meaning is far from a theoretical matter. It requires a search for modes of institutional and corporate life in which biblical discourse is trusted and competently used. Indeed, it may well be that the breakdown of the primacy of Scripture in the church and in theology has its roots not only in (for example) the prestige of certain understandings of historical-critical methods but also in what has been called "a failure of socialization."[5] And further, it may well be that renewed attention to the Bible will be secured first and foremost not by better theoretical arguments concerning its nature or the mode of its production but by "the actual, fruitful use religious people continue to make of it in ways which enhance their own and other people's lives."[6] Learning how to "inhabit" Scripture in these ways is a matter of catechesis, of an intense need to relearn what it means to think and speak as people of the gospel, and thus as people whose perceptions and habits of discourse are governed by the scriptural testimony to the gospel.

But there is a further answer to the question of why we may find the frankly theological tenor of my proposal rather strange. Talking theologically about the Bible as Holy Scripture, or using the language of Spirit and faith to prescribe how the Bible is to be read, locates this text and the acts through which we interpret it in a specific place: the cultural region of Christian faith. However, one of the most important shifts in modernity makes it acutely difficult for us to think in such territorial terms. That shift is the decline of local hermeneutical cultures. The interpretation of texts, that is, has commonly been extracted from particular communities of interpretation and

5. Kathryn Tanner, *God and Creation in Christian Theology: Tyranny or Empowerment?* (Oxford: Blackwell, 1988), 169.

6. Hans Frei, "The 'Literal Reading' of Biblical Narrative in the Christian Tradition: Does It Stretch or Will It Break?," in *The Bible and the Narrative Tradition*, ed. Frank McConnell (Oxford: Oxford University Press, 1986), 36–77, at 37.

standardized. Local hermeneutical practice has become subordinate
to general theory, and general theory has been expounded in such a
way that it alone furnishes the norms for what ought to happen in
any particular field of reading.[7]

What are the effects of this on Christian reading of the Bible? First,
and most obviously, it has issued in the gradual decline of theological
description of what happens when the church reads the Bible. It is not
merely that modern academic convention demands that the Bible be
read "like any other book." In itself, that is not a particularly damaging convention, if all that is meant is that the Bible really is a *text* (of
course, more is usually meant). What is much more problematic is
the naturalization not just of the text but of the entire hermeneutical situation. When the situation of reading the Bible is no longer
Christianly construed as an episode in God's dealings with God's
people, as part of the process whereby God arrests our ignorance
of his ways and savingly communicates with us, then theological
description is superfluous: it doesn't take us to the heart of what is
happening when we read this book. In fact, the hermeneutical situation comes to be seen as a historical undertaking which can best be
understood by appealing to general principles and norms of explanation. Language about God can safely be retired or, at least, pushed
to the margins of hermeneutical description, since it adds nothing
of any real referential force to our account of what we are about.

Second, the decline of local hermeneutics and the expansion of general theory goes hand in hand with a prioritizing of "understanding"
over "use." What Paul Ricoeur called the "de-regionalization" of
hermeneutics involves the elaboration of a universal theory of "understanding" which can be made to embrace all occurrences.[8] Such a
theory tends to be largely asocial and acontextual, subsuming all
particulars under a transcendental notion of understanding whose
core is anthropology. In this, understanding a text is envisaged as a

7. See Francis Watson, "The Scope of Hermeneutics," in *The Cambridge Companion to Christian Doctrine*, ed. Colin E. Gunton (Cambridge: Cambridge University
Press, 1997), 65–80.

8. Paul Ricoeur, "The Task of Hermeneutics," in *Hermeneutics and the Human
Sciences: Essays on Language, Action and Interpretation*, ed. John B. Thompson
(Cambridge: Cambridge University Press, 1981), 43–62, at 44.

phenomenon which is stable across a great range of instances; it is not an ability or practice of particular persons in particular situations with particular ends in view.[9]

Third, and for our present theme most important, the elaboration of general hermeneutics tends to demote "biblical theology" (that is, theology controlled by the scriptural text) to inferior status, since such theology is merely local. Only that which transcends all particular spaces and uses may make a claim on our reason. Biblical theology—theology which happens in this region and is subservient to this text—cannot pretend to be anything other than a bit of local geography. The point is made with great force by Kant in his 1797 essay *The Conflict of the Faculties*. Here a very sharp distinction is drawn between what is established on the basis of reason and what derives from the merely positive or statutory authority of a text. So, Kant writes, "The biblical theologian (as a member of a higher faculty) draws his teaching not from reason but from the *Bible*."[10] The member of the philosophical faculty, however, can aspire to universality, since he or she stands beneath no statutes and is bound to no locality. If the biblical theologian should begin to "meddle with his reason," then he simply steps outside of his sphere, leaping, Kant says, "over the wall of ecclesiastical faith, the only thing that assures his salvation, and strays into the free and open fields of private judgment and philosophy."[11] The spatial metaphor here is telling: the biblical theologian's ecclesiastical faith always takes place in protective confinement, behind a wall; the philosopher, by contrast, wanders freely in open fields. For Kant, we note, locality always means constriction. A little later, the contrast is phrased slightly differently. "A biblical theologian is, properly speaking, one *versed in the Scriptures*

9. See here Stephen E. Fowl and L. Gregory Jones, *Reading in Communion: Scripture and Ethics in Christian Life* (Grand Rapids: Eerdmans, 1991); Charles M. Wood, *The Formation of Christian Understanding: An Essay in Theological Hermeneutics* (Philadelphia: Westminster, 1981); Gerald L. Bruns, *Inventions: Writing, Textuality, and Understanding in Literary History* (New Haven: Yale University Press, 1982). By way of contrast, see the work of Werner G. Jeanrond, *Text and Interpretation as Categories of Theological Thinking* (Dublin: Gill & Macmillan, 1988) and *Theological Hermeneutics: Development and Significance* (London: SCM, 1994).

10. Immanuel Kant, *The Conflict of the Faculties* (Lincoln: University of Nebraska Press, 1992), 35.

11. Kant, *Conflict*, 37.

with regard to *ecclesiastical faith*, which is based on statutes—that is, on laws proceeding from another person's act of choice. A rational theologian, on the other hand, is one *versed in reason* with regard to *religious faith*, which is based on inner laws that can be developed from every man's own reason."[12] Once again, the force of Kant's argument is to denigrate that which is merely local (*this* text, *this* community, *this* authoritative tradition) in favor of a picture of the undetermined self whose center is universal reason. One could portray large tracts of the history of modern theology out of this paradigmatic contrast between statute and reason. Such a history might show, for instance, that one of the driving forces behind the much-lamented separation of biblical and theological studies is the assumption that biblical theology cannot claim to be anything other than merely the exegesis and application of local statutes. Once that assumption acquires prestige, then theology can find itself between a rock and a hard place: either retreat back behind the wall of ecclesiastical faith or reinvent theology as a philosophical discipline.

I want to suggest that these are not the only options and that we do well to consider reentering the local hermeneutical culture of the Christian gospel, rearticulating some of its major features, namely a certain theological account of Scripture and its reading and, as a consequence, reappropriating certain rhetorical strategies on the part of Christian theology. It is, therefore, incumbent upon us to offer a rich, judicious, and, above all, theologically alert depiction of the elements of the hermeneutical culture of Christian faith, in all its elements: text, church, reader, and most of all the living eloquent God of the gospel. Once this is done and we have attained the right measure of Christian determinacy and descriptive depth in our account, then things may begin to fall into place. We may, perhaps, begin to see that Kant's rather dismal statutory faith and his stolid biblical theologians have very little to do with the practices of astonishment which make up Christian eschatological culture and its hearing of the Word. And so it is to depiction of those practices of astonishment that we now give our attention, looking in turn at Scripture, reading, and the rhetoric of theology.

12. Kant, *Conflict*, 61.

Holy Scripture is the Word of God in which the people of God are overwhelmed by a summons to obedience to the gospel.

A good deal hangs on locating a theological account of the Bible in the right doctrinal place. Indeed, the force of an argument like that which Kant makes in *The Conflict of the Faculties* is—as we shall see—considerably lessened once we see that it trades upon a doctrinal mislocation of Scripture (a mislocation into which, of course, post-Reformation Protestantism had already fallen well before Kant's time). The proper doctrinal location for a Christian theological account of Scripture is (primarily) in the doctrine of the Trinity and (secondarily and derivatively) in the doctrine of the church. A theology of Holy Scripture is not about establishing *a priori* whether and how God may speak, nor is it about the exercise of ecclesial authority, but about the posterior depiction of who is the God who speaks and who are those whom God addresses. For such depiction, trinitarian and ecclesiological doctrine is basic.

One of the functions of the doctrine of the Trinity is to ensure a fully *theocentric* account of how it is that we know God. Trinitarian doctrine is, in part, a way of articulating how the entire process of the church's knowledge of God is God's own work, the work of Father, Son, and Spirit. Knowledge of God originates not in creaturely aspiration but in the will of the Father, whose absolute freedom is directed outward in self-communication with his creatures. Knowledge of God is effected not by creaturely acts but by God's self-utterance as "Word" in the Son who is the embodied declaration of the Father's will to manifest himself. Knowledge of God is made real to the creature not in some self-wrought act of self-understanding on the creature's part but in the work of the Spirit who renders the will and Word of God efficacious by himself establishing hearing and obedience. Thus knowledge of God—obedient fellowship with God who is the truth—is the work of the undivided Trinity, willing, effecting, and realizing such fellowship in the miracle of self-utterance. This miracle generates the church. God's act of revelation does not occur "to" the church, as if "church" preexists God's self-utterance; rather, "church" is what comes to be as this utterance occurs in a majestic and sovereign initiative. Once again: church is the eschatological reality of the new creation; it is the "creature of the Word." And as creature, the church is simply not competent to receive the Word, let alone to authorize it. In the Word, the church hears God's summons to obedient attention to the gospel.

Where does Holy Scripture as text fit into this trinitarian and ecclesiological account of divine self-communication? Very simply: Holy Scripture is the means or instrument through which the mortifying and vivifying self-manifestation of God addresses the church, slaying and making alive. In and through this text, God makes the gospel into a commanding presence. Holy Scripture disturbs. Precisely as the medium of God's holiness, it is a rock thrown in our path, an onslaught which smites our idolatries and us as idolaters. In this text we are arrested and addressed by God. The text of Scripture is a permanent protest against the tendency of Christian culture to "de-eschatologize" itself and its condition, that is, to convert the presence of God into "what may be touched" and thereby to refuse to stand beneath the sign of its own contradiction. Kafka once wrote: "I think we ought to read only books that bite and sting us. If the book we are reading doesn't shake us awake like a blow on the skull, why bother reading it in the first place? . . . A book must be the axe for the frozen sea within us."[13] It is because we are bitten or stung by God through the biblical text that we talk of the "authority" of Scripture.

To speak of Scripture's authority is not to indicate something which is "statutory"; it is to acknowledge *God's use* of the text. God's use is not our use. "Functionalist" accounts of the authority of the Bible, which construe it in terms of the text's capacity to enable the identity and duration of ecclesial process, are characteristically weak at this point. Their elaboration of the tasks which the Bible accomplishes in the Christian community needs to be undergirded by an account of Scripture as an instrument through which God acts upon (and, crucially, *against*) the church. To speak of the authority of Scripture simply by recounting its ecclesial uses is inadequate whenever

13. Alberto Manguel, *A History of Reading* (London: HarperCollins, 1996), 93. [Manguel quotes Kafka's words to his friend and classmate Oskar Pollak in a letter dated January 27, 1904.]

it suggests that the Bible's normative role derives from those uses, rather than that the uses are in the end contingent upon something else—the prevenience and authority of the God of the gospel, present to the church in the power of the Holy Spirit.

In Christian theology, the authority of Scripture must be based not only in the social practice of forming a canon, which it shares with other communities, but in acknowledging God's unique activity in the formation and interpretation of Scripture. For theological purposes, the crucial point is not that authority of Scripture is political but that it is divine. Not only does the community affirm that these stories are *about* God, but that they are *of* God, and therefore capable of sustaining Christ's church. And it is because God has disclosed himself in these stories that they have hegemony over other stories. The whole of reality (including other stories) must be read into the Christian narrative, not simply because all of us are bound by the contexts of our irreducible sociolinguistic frameworks, but because God commands the church to be about this business. In the Christian case, the extension of the communal narrative is a divine *requirement*.[14]

The authority of Scripture is properly a matter for the church's *acknowledgment* rather than the church's *ascription*; otherwise, we may so emphasize the location of Scripture within the processes of ecclesial life that its *critical* power is compromised. A text which simply confirmed existing thought, speech, and action would not be Holy Scripture in the Christian sense, for it would no longer be about the business of initiating a crisis by exposing the life of the church to interruption and judgment.

14. On this see further David H. Kelsey, "The Bible and Christian Theology," *Journal of the American Academy of Religion* 48 (1980): 385–402, esp. 396. [Webster's original typescript and the text of the lecture as published in *Stimulus* 6, no. 4 (1998), 10–16, at 13, both mark this entire paragraph ("In Christian theology . . . divine *requirement*") as a quotation from Kelsey's article, but the passage appears instead to be Webster's own words, as influenced by Kelsey: it is presented as such in the version of the lecture published as John Webster, "Scripture, Reading, and the Rhetoric of Theology in Hans Frei's Analysis of Texts," in *Ten Year Commemoration to the Life of Hans Frei (1922–1988)*, ed. Giorgy Olegovich (New York: Semenenko Foundation, 1999), 41–53, at 47–48.]

So far, then, I have suggested that the Bible is one of the elements which compose the particular field of action, the local hermeneutical culture of Christian faith. That field is described by offering an account of identity and action of the self-revealing, Triune God, of the church as the assembly which is evoked and sustained in life by God's speech, and of the text as the instrument appropriated by God to confront the church with the gospel. What, next, does it mean to be a hearer and reader of this text?

It is more important to lay out an anthropology of the reader than to establish a set of methodological directives for reading. In theological portraiture of this local hermeneutical culture, the questions of greatest consequence do not concern the sort of interpretative tactics which are to be adopted in face of this text; the key issues are rather: "What sort of person am I to be as I read this text? What sort of person does this text invite me or compel me to become?" Considered in and of themselves, methods are of only penultimate significance, subservient to the construal that we have of the context of their deployment and of particular readers who are deploying them. Certainly, our construal of the situation may lead us to decide that certain methods are preferable, and others of only subordinate significance or no significance at all. Methods of reading which accord a high degree of autonomy to readers and reading communities, for instance, are unlikely to prove compatible with strong affirmations of the text as a mediator of (rather than mere occasion for) divine acts of speech. But, in the end, a choice for or against this or that method will be determined by wider considerations (however much those considerations remain subterranean in most discussions of hermeneutical method). Included among these considerations will be anthropological commitments, and especially understandings of human freedom and competence in coming to understand the text.

The Christian reader of Holy Scripture is located within the eschatological situation as we have been attempting to portray it. This already means that the reader is not just a mind before which a passive text appears. Reading in this region is an act in response to God's act of speaking through the text of the Bible to the people of God. It is caught up into the struggle of sin and redemption which embraces all human history and action. Reading the Bible is an event in this history. This is not to deny that readers must, indeed, go to work on the text of the Bible; it is not utterly transparent, asking nothing but to be absorbed by an utterly passive listener. But as the reader struggles to read, the application of the history of salvation takes place. Idolatry is reproved; repentance is commanded and generated by the Spirit; fresh obedience is secured. This dynamic defines the Christian reader of the Bible; Christian acts of reading Holy Scripture are encounters between the gracious, eloquent God of the gospel and the sinner who has been arrested and made new.

All this is involved in being what Calvin calls a "pupil" of Scripture, one who applies him- or herself "teachably to God's Word."[15] Such reading is outside the range of our natural competence, for the reader's capacities are distorted by "insensibility," that is, a hardness or resistance which makes us unwilling to hear and all too willing to manipulate. The teachableness which characterizes properly ordered reading involves a certain passivity: respect, receptivity, readiness to be confronted, and, above all, humility. Overthrown by the address of God, the reader is reoriented, re-established, and made capable of directing him- or herself to the end of hearing God's Word. Reading the Bible is an incident in the baptismal process of mortification and vivification, of overthrow and re-establishment; anything less would not match up to the eschatological character of Christian reading.

With this we may return to Kant. Kant's misperception of the matter lies partly in the fact that he cannot think of the Bible as other than the oppressive domestic statutes of the ecclesiastical community. For him, the scriptural writings are merely "teachings that proceed from an act of choice on the part of an authority."[16] Scripture has here become detached from the communicative divine act in which human darkness is invaded by the light of the gospel; the eschatological idiom within which alone it makes sense to talk of Holy Scripture has been replaced by the language of Scripture as an organ of petty social control. But there is more to Kant's animus against biblical theology; it is undergirded by an anthropology whose constitutive moment is what the benighted biblical theologian can see only as "the ill-reputed spirit of

15. John Calvin, *Institutes of the Christian Religion*, ed. John T. McNeill, trans. Ford Lewis Battles (Philadelphia: Westminster, 1960), I.vi.2, at 72.
16. Kant, *Conflict*, 33.

freedom that belongs to reason and philosophy."[17] As so often since the
early modern period, "freedom" and "text" run in opposed directions.
Moving beyond Kant, I suggest, requires revisiting the notion that God
makes use of this text, redescribing it in order to give it a properly Christian content and so to dissociate it from the politics of repression. But
it also requires a different anthropology, one in which there is a proper
dignity to repentant listening. Lastly, it also demands that we give some
deliberate attention to the relationship of theological discourse to the
text of Scripture, which is our final task in today's lecture.

⟾·◇·⟽

Theology seeks to persuade. Like all discourses, theological discourse
attempts to engage its readers in such a way as to modify beliefs and
attitudes, and so influence behavior. The rhetoric of theological texts
is the means whereby they position themselves in front of the reader
in such a way as to maximize their effect and thereby shape the reader
in a deeper and more enduring way. "Rhetoric" here is used in a very
wide sense, referring not simply to selection and use of language
but to the entire strategy of persuasion: genre, use of authorities,
conformity or otherwise to shared assumptions and expectations,
as well as modes of address. All scholarly discourse, including the
discourse of theology, is rhetoric. We are, of course, customarily
more conscious of the rhetoric of texts from ages and cultures not
our own, precisely because their lack of fit with our own norms serves
to highlight their distinctiveness. The rhetorical devices of Luther's
Babylonian Captivity of the Church or of Newman's *Grammar of
Assent* are evident to us; those of a modern biblical commentary or
theological monograph are less so.

Yet modern scholarly theology has its own rhetoric—even (precisely)
at its most dispassionate, it is an exercise in the formation of dispositions and actions. The formation is undertaken by modes of argument
which appeal to the reader as one possessed of reason, reserved and
unattached to any particular version of reality, one for whom assent
follows from sober weighing of evidence, cumulatively presented so as
to appeal to the mind's judgment. One of the implications is that their

17. Kant, *Conflict*, 37.

rhetorical strategies are interest free, nonlocal, and therefore applicable to any intellectual sphere, for their home is in the modern university, that institution where unbiased reason does its daily work. The combined efforts of the genealogical, hermeneutical, and linguistic turns (that is, of Nietzsche, Heidegger, and Wittgenstein) have, of course, served to disabuse us of the totalizing pretensions of modern scholarly discourse by laying bare the political dimensions of its instrumentalism. Some theological versions of that critique have issued in a pragmatism or relativism which we may judge to be corrosive. Nevertheless, it serves to indicate something of quite crucial significance for any account of the rhetoric of theology: persuasion is a local art.

What kinds of rhetoric are fitting in the eschatological culture of Christian faith and theology? Two features seem to me of particular importance: the *rhetoric of effacement* and the *rhetoric of edification*. First, the rhetoric of effacement. Basic to Christian eschatological culture is attention to the gospel as something sheerly unmanageable and surprising. Attention dispossesses us of our expectations; it involves self-renunciation so that the gospel itself may speak of its own presence and vitality. Holy Scripture is the announcement of the eschatological gospel, and it is in attentive, ascetic reading of Scripture that the gospel is pressed upon the attention of the people of God. *Christian theology is the repetition in the movement of thought of this attentive, ascetic reading.* The concepts and language of Christian theology "repeat" the act of reading Scripture, that is, they are the transposition into reflective terms of the abandonment which is the essence of attentiveness, of hearing: hence hearing is a matter of habits of *ascesis*. The aim of this transposition is to draw up a map of the kinds of readings of the Bible which best promote the sovereignty of the gospel in the church. Theology is (to continue the cartographic metaphor) a projection which enables readers of Scripture to find their way around the biblical worlds. This is why (as Barth put it in his book on Anselm) theological *intelligere* means nothing other than "to read and ponder what has already been said"; that is, theology is "no more than a deepened form of *legere*."[18] To

18. Karl Barth, *Anselm: Fides Quaerens Intellectum; Anselm's Proof of the Existence of God in the Context of His Theological Scheme* (London: SCM, 1960), 40–41.

be sure, it is *deepened legere*: there is a proper level of theological reflection which is not to be collapsed into the more immediate activities of faith's apprehension of the *Credo*. But what is crucial here is that, as the understanding of faith, theology is not superior to "what has already been said," nor is it about the business of inquiry into its possibility or necessity. Its task is more modest and restricted. Theology has the function of enabling the church to be the *ecclesia audiens*, assisting competent reading and reception of Scripture. As such, it is a summons to attentiveness, a reminder that, because the use of the Bible is always threatened by domestication, the church has always to *begin again* with Scripture. Theology is thus most properly an invitation to read and reread Scripture, to hear and be caught up by Scripture's challenge to a repentant, nonmanipulative heeding of God's Word.

It is, therefore, of prime importance to avoid construing theology as a set of improvements upon Scripture. The necessity of the theoretical language of theology should not blind us to the fact that it is exposed to the "heresy of paraphrase"—the heresy, that is, of thinking that theology, once formulated, effectively replaces the more rudimentary language forms of the Bible.[19] It is fatally easy to prefer the relatively clean lines of theology to the much less manageable, untheorized material of the Bible. But once we begin to do that, theology quickly becomes a way of easing ourselves of some permanently troubling tracts of Christian language: in effect, theology's rhetoric serves to de-eschatologize the church's apprehension of the gospel. What is required in an account of theology and its rhetoric is something much more lightweight, low-level, and approximate, something therefore less likely to compete with or displace Scripture as the testimony to that around which Christian faith is organized. Thus modesty and transparency are the hallmarks of theology's rhetoric. In effect, this means that theology operates best when it is a kind of gloss on Scripture—a discursive reiteration or indication of the truth of the

19. David Tracy, *The Analogical Imagination: Christian Theology and the Culture of Pluralism* (London: SCM, 1981), 293n57. See also George Lindbeck's protest against "translation theology" in "Scripture, Consensus, and Community," in *Biblical Interpretation in Crisis: The Ratzinger Conference on Bible and Church*, ed. Richard John Neuhaus (Grand Rapids: Eerdmans, 1989), 74–101, at 87–88.

Christian gospel as it is encountered in the Bible. Above all, what is required is an understanding of the nature of theology which is self-effacing, in which the function of theology is exhausted in the role it plays vis-à-vis Scripture. "The Church's dogmatic activity, its attempts to structure its public and common language in such a way that the possibilities of judgment and renewal are not buried, must constantly be chastened by the awareness that it so acts in order to give place to the freedom of God—the freedom of God from the Church's sense of itself and its power, and thus the freedom of God to renew and absolve."[20] If theology has to do with "giving place to the freedom of God," then its rhetoric must be modest enough to demonstrate and encourage attentiveness to Scripture.

Second, the rhetoric of edification. One of the central tasks of Christian theology is to generate persuasive depictions of Christian faith. This is by no means the sole task which Christian theology is required to perform. Theology is not only a descriptive exercise; it has critical functions to perform. Nevertheless, a theology which seeks to follow the movement of the prophetic and apostolic witness of Scripture cannot but be engaged in depiction (and, as we shall come to see in a later lecture, one of the conditions for the success of its critical work will be the accuracy and depth of its descriptions). For this reason we need to exercise some caution in drawing rather sharp distinctions between "Christian practice" and "Christian theology," or between "first-order" activities such as proclamation and prayer and "second-order" activities such as theological reflection. Such distinctions are frequently made by contemporary theologians, sometimes to ensure the subordination of theology to the practices of faith, sometimes to ensure that theological reflection is kept free to perform a critical, anti-ideological role. In these contexts, the distinction is no doubt important, but in its more sharply defined versions it would be almost unrecognizable to many classical Christian writers, for whom the difference between "first-order" and "second-order" did not exist.

Theology in the classical mold was centrally (though not, of course, exclusively) concerned with the instruction, guidance, and formation

20. Rowan Williams, "The Incarnation as the Basis of Dogma," in *The Religion of the Incarnation*, ed. Robert Morgan (Bristol: Bristol Classical Press, 1989), 85–98, at 89.

of the disciples of Jesus Christ. The American theologian Ellen Charry has called this the "salutarity" principle: theological doctrine is "aretegenic" in that it has the pastoral task of seeking to cultivate virtue and thereby to edify. "Christian doctrines function pastorally when a theologian unearths the divine pedagogy in order to engage the reader or listener in considering that life with the triune God facilitates dignity and excellence."[21] How does this affect the rhetoric of theology? It is not simply a matter of adding pious flourishes to soften the severe lines of formal theological discussion (plenty of modern theological texts do that). Still less is it a matter of abandoning theology to whatever practical issues happen to have found their way to the top of the church's agenda. It is rather a matter of recognition that, in following God's address of the church in Holy Scripture, theology cannot be anything other than a commendation of the gospel.

There are implications here for the genres of theological writing. A good deal of classical Christian theology was written as commentary, paraphrase, or reflection upon major texts in the tradition—primarily biblical texts, but also by derivation creedal or other writings of sufficient stature and durability to constitute permanently enriching statements of the gospel. Modern theology has largely lost touch with this genre. The biblical commentary has by and large become the repository of linguistic, historical, and literary comment; modern commentaries on creedal texts are often little more than free reflection organized under the headings of the confession. One of the primary reasons for the decline of the genre of running paraphrase of or expansion upon classics (biblical or otherwise) is that the genre does not sit easily with the anti-statutory tendency of modernity which has deeply shaped scholarly rhetoric and which makes these older genres scarcely recognizable as intellectual discourse. They are deliberately unoriginal. They start *in media res* and not *de novo* and do not accept that "recital" and "creativity" are necessarily antithetical.[22] They are

21. Ellen Charry, *By the Renewing of Your Mind: The Pastoral Function of Christian Doctrine* (Oxford: Oxford University Press, 1997), 18. See also Serene Jones, *Calvin and the Rhetoric of Piety* (Louisville: Westminster John Knox, 1995), and William C. Placher, *The Domestication of Transcendence: How Modern Thinking about God Went Wrong* (Louisville: Westminster John Knox, 1996), 52–68.

22. See the comments on the *florilegium* by Jaroslav Pelikan, *The Vindication of Tradition* (New Haven: Yale University Press, 1984), 74–75.

noncritical, in that they demonstrate rather little interest in giving an account of the historical genesis of that upon which they comment. Their relationship to the language of the Bible and its derivative dialects is prior to its relation to the language of high culture or philosophy. And they are unsystematic, in that they eschew reorganizing their material, preferring to let its own logic stand without submitting it to pressure to conform to external schemes. Above all, they seek to guide by teaching, and therefore the response which their rhetoric invites is affective and moral as much as intellectual. "The eloquent divine," says Augustine, seeks to "subdue the will . . . by the power of eloquence."[23] If these features are strange to us, may it not be that we find ourselves at a distance, not only from earlier habits of theological discourse, but from the Christian cultural attachments within terms of which these habits made sense and could flourish?

What conclusions can be drawn from all this? One very brief and not wholly frivolous comment upon which to end. Theologians should consider ceasing to write systematic treatises and confine themselves to the work of exposition of Scripture. In his somewhat rollicking comments on university education in the 1520 treatise *To the Christian Nobility of the German Nation*, Luther urged that

> the writings of all the holy fathers should be read only for a time so that through them we may be led into the Scriptures. As it is, however, we only read them these days to avoid going any further and getting into the Bible. We are like men who read the sign posts and never travel the road they indicate. Our dear fathers wanted to lead us to the Scriptures by their writings, but we use their works to get away from the Scriptures. Nevertheless, the Scripture alone is our vineyard in which we must all labour and toil.[24]

That, I suggest, is how it should be.

---

23. Augustine, *On Christian Doctrine* (Edinburgh: T&T Clark, 1873), IV.13.29. See Thomas F. Martin, "'An Abundant Supply of Discourse': Augustine and the Rhetoric of Monasticism," *Downside Review* 116, no. 402 (January 1998): 7–25.
24. Martin Luther, *Three Treatises* (Philadelphia: Fortress, 1970), 98.

3

Traditions

Theology and the Public Covenant

THOSE OF YOU WHO ARE TEMPTED to write me off as some sort of apocalyptic lunatic may be a bit surprised by the theme of this lecture, which is the relation of theology to tradition. For although "tradition" and "eschatology" are often thought to be antithetical concepts, I want to suggest that Christian theology of the kind I'm recommending is inseparable from the apostolic tradition. But I also want to suggest that when we talk of the Christian tradition as "apostolic," we aren't referring so much backward as upward: the tradition is apostolic because its impulse is in the sheer freedom with which God calls and sends.

My subtitle—theology and the public covenant—echoes some words from one of the classic texts of modern religious thought, Kant's *Religion within the Limits of Reason Alone*.[1] In the course of this remarkably austere and morally demanding work, Kant reads the situation of religion and theology in the modern era by means of a contrast between "pure religion" and what he calls "historical"

1. Immanuel Kant, *Religion within the Limits of Reason Alone* (New York: Harper & Row, 1960).

81

or "ecclesiastical faith." Pure religion (which he also calls "rational faith") is concerned with moral obedience, the fulfillment of the duty to conform ourselves to an idea of moral perfection "which reason presents to us for our zealous emulation."[2] Such religion is a religion from which everything external is excluded with unsparing rigor. Kant is utterly scrupulous in wanting to detach this pure form of moral religion from any tangible, historical forms. Whether it be the trappings of religious culture or public worship as a direct, embodied transaction between God and moral subject or the public history of Jesus himself: all simply constitute concessions to the human need for what is "*sensibly tenable*," and so all compromise the pure rational character of moral religion.[3] Such concessions to the tangible, however, are the stuff of statutory "ecclesiastical faith," which, Kant says, "requires a *public* covenant"—what we might perhaps call a socially embodied tradition. Inevitably, therefore, ecclesiastical faith renounces the internality and universality which are proper to rational religion. "The common man," Kant writes, "always takes [religion] to mean his ecclesiastical faith, which appeals to his senses, whereas religion is hidden within and has to do with moral dispositions."[4] The kind of antithesis which Kant draws between moral-religious interiority and public covenants has haunted discussion of theology's relation to the Christian tradition in modernity, and much of what I want to say today is a critical response to what he has to say.

The nature and place of "tradition" is one of the central issues in analyzing the situation of modernity. Around the concept cluster all manner of moral, political, and intellectual ideals, and the defense or repudiation of tradition is one of the markers by which we may map out competing accounts of the state of modern culture. The issues which surround the so-called detraditionalization of modern societies are complex and contested, and analysis is often hindered by the predominance of the merely anecdotal or impressionistic.[5]

2. Kant, *Religion within the Limits of Reason Alone*, 54.
3. Kant, *Religion within the Limits of Reason Alone*, 100.
4. Kant, *Religion within the Limits of Reason Alone*, 99.
5. For what follows, see Paul Heelas, Scott Lash, and Paul Morris, eds., *Detraditionalization: Critical Reflections on Authority and Identity* (Oxford: Blackwell, 1996).

One (strong or radical) thesis argues that tradition has ceased to play a role in modern societies; pregiven orders have been replaced by disembedded, contingent modes of life characterized by openness and choice, in which the customary and communal no longer hold sway. The reasons advanced for the decline of tradition are varied: the technologization of modern life, the accessibility of a vast range of differentiated cultural resources, the construction of mass consumerism by capitalism. The result is a fundamental shift in human identity in which self-realizing subjectivity in the present becomes axiomatic. Another, rather different, thesis argues that tradition and modernity are not necessarily opposed concepts. Traditional societies are not, in fact, as stable and objective in orientation as might be supposed, and modern, supposedly detraditionalized, societies retain elements of competing traditions. On this latter account, it is a considerable overstatement to claim that modern cultures are entirely adrift from tradition; in effect, tradition and detraditionalization co-exist.

A number of recent accounts of the theological task gravitate toward the radical thesis just mentioned. Something like that thesis governs their historical analysis of modern theology (which suffers from being cut adrift from its moorings) and their normative proposals (theology is the self-articulation of the Christian tradition, not its critical inspection). Such theologies take courage from the rehabilitation of tradition across a number of different fields of inquiry, especially from the turn away from critical philosophy and the modes of intellectual practice of which it formed a commanding example, and from liberal individualism in politics and morals.[6] For reasons set out in the first lecture, I have a good deal of sympathy with this account; I do not think theology can be detached from the public covenant of ecclesiastical faith. Yet the issue is not tradition per se but *this* tradition.

It is of crucial significance that we develop an account of tradition which is decisively shaped by theological factors, one, that is, whose primary impulse derives from the content of Christian faith, rather

---

6. Delwin Brown, *Boundaries of Our Habitations: Tradition and Theological Construction* (Albany, NY: SUNY Press, 1994); David L. Gross, *The Past in Ruins: Tradition and the Critique of Modernity* (Amherst: University of Massachusetts Press, 1992).

than from general considerations of the constitutive role of traditions
in human life and thought. What is it about *this* public covenant—
which we have earlier talked about as the eschatological culture of
Christian faith—which gives a particular shape to the relation of faith
and tradition? Much hangs on achieving the right kind of Christian
specificity here. Most of all, on this depends the capacity of Christian theology to articulate a coherent and persuasive response to the
critique of the notion of tradition which Kant and others pressed with
such sharpness and which continues to accompany its rehabilitation
in the present: namely, the criticism that tradition means closure. My
suggestion, toward the end of this lecture, is that a distinctively theological account of the public covenant of Christianity undermines
the de-eschatologizing potential of tradition; in fact, a theological
account of tradition is a matter of tracing the permanent revolution
to which the gospel gives rise.

⇒◆⇐

As I am using the term here, "tradition" is a theological, rather than
simply a sociocultural or political, concept. As such, it is best articulated in terms of the fourth mark of the church, namely apostolicity,
which in turn is itself best set forth by an account of the presence of
Jesus to the church in the power of the Holy Spirit.

The need for an account such as this can readily be illustrated. Its
lack is especially evident in the work of those (postliberal) theologians who draw heavily on categories developed in social anthropology in formulating a theory of Christianity. One of the most strik-
ing features of some postliberal theology is that a *formal* proposal
about the tradition-constituted ("cultural-linguistic") character of
religion rather quickly becomes a *material* proposal about the content of Christianity. Ecclesial process comes to occupy center stage
in the depiction of what Christianity is. The problem here is not—as
many less attentive critics of the work of Lindbeck, for example,
allege—that a focus on the ecclesial leads to sectarianism: clearly
in his case it does not.[7] Nor is the problem simply that investment

7. David H. Kelsey, "Church Discourse and Public Realm," in *Theology and Dialogue: Essays in Conversation with George Lindbeck*, ed. Bruce D. Marshall (Notre
Dame, IN: University of Notre Dame Press, 1990), 7–33.

in the metaphors of "grammar" or "culture" to talk about religion can overstress regularity and undervalue the dis-equilibrium which can characterize religious traditions, especially those with a strong eschatological component. The greatest problem is that a certain *doctrinal* configuration tends to be presupposed in some postliberal theology, one in which ecclesiology shifts to the center and in which language about the presence of Christ and of the agency of the Holy Spirit tends to be occluded or accorded only background status. The critical energy of much postliberalism, especially in its repudiation of liberal, correlationist, or "experiential-expressivist" theology, derives clearly enough from Barth (though often a Barth shorn of some tracts of his doctrine of revelation); but its disposition of doctrines is in many respects much closer to Schleiermacher, for whom "Dogmatic Theology is the science which systematizes the doctrine prevalent in a Christian Church at a given time."[8] In the absence of robust, operative language of the economic actions of the Holy Trinity, something central is missed in theological depiction of tradition as the "public covenant" of Christianity.

A rather different problem can be traced in the work of others whose account of the public covenant of Christianity owes much less to descriptive social anthropology and much more to postmodern critical theory of culture. A very compelling recent example here is the work of Kathryn Tanner, where she presses the idea that tradition is a *construct*. She writes, "'Tradition' is always a selection from the wide array of materials that could be so designated in virtue of their transmission from before and elsewhere. . . . Tradition is always a matter of human attribution; nothing about the materials themselves requires that designation. Even ongoing customary forms of action and belief do not constitute a tradition until they are marked as such and thereby assigned a normative status."[9] The point is well taken: as we will see later on in this lecture, the notion of tradition, like the notion of culture, must not be abstracted from the political processes of its production and authorization. Yet a measure of arbitrariness can

8. Friedrich Schleiermacher, *The Christian Faith* (Edinburgh: T&T Clark, 1928), 88.

9. Kathryn Tanner, *Theories of Culture: A New Agenda for Theology* (Minneapolis: Fortress, 1997), 133.

be generated by this resistance to any naive notion of the givenness of the contents of a tradition. And, even more important, there is a principled minimalism in Tanner's language about God, reminiscent of the austerity of Kant but usually stated in Tanner's fairly frequent references to Barth's insistence throughout his work that the divine freedom means that God is not an available object within a tradition. The problem here is not that Tanner eschews appeal to Christian doctrine in her account of tradition; though the book does invest heavily in postmodern cultural theory, the argument is also under-pinned by a (rather severely) apophatic doctrine of God. But it is just this doctrine which proves problematic. So strict is it in refusing any identification of divine action within the processes of tradition that language of the communicative presence of the risen and ascended Christ, and of the Spirit's presence in and through the church, is in some measure eclipsed. The reasons for that—the need for critical purchase against the inflation of tradition—are entirely laudable. But it is worth asking whether the same end cannot be attained without submitting to such a prohibitive regime of restrictions.

How, then, might we develop a doctrinal account of the Christian tradition in order to prepare for some reflection on the role of theology within it? Tradition concerns the relation of past and present; one of the chief functions of the notion of tradition is to enable us to articulate how the originating event of Christianity relates to the activities in the present which we call Christian faith or disciple-ship. "The question of tradition is the question of time, and of the way we live in it. One's conception of tradition therefore depends on one's concept of time."[10]

How are we to think about the temporal gap between Jesus and the contemporary reality of Christian faith? One way—again, much in favor with postmodern theology—is to see the gap between then and now as filled with a fluid play of readings and interpretations. The historical space between Jesus and ourselves is crammed with sets of cultural negotiations and thus is to be seen as an essentially political or aesthetic process, ungoverned or only marginally governed

10. Colin E. Gunton, *A Brief Theology of Revelation* (Edinburgh: T&T Clark, 1995), 87.

by any established instruments of identity and continuity. We could call this "tradition as play." Another way would be to see tradition as the "effective history" of the originating event of Christianity in which that event is "realized." On this account of matters, Jesus's history remains abstract or merely "objective" until made real through traditions of human life and action.

Both those ways of thinking of the relation of Jesus's past to our present tend to perpetuate the assumption that there is, indeed, a distance between Jesus and ourselves, and that the distance has to be bridged, as it were, from our end. That is, they start from the assumption that, as a past figure, he is absent, and that it is the job of tradition to compensate for that absence. There is a doctrinal deficiency here, and it is christological and pneumatological. It is a repetition of the problem which has had such an adverse effect on modern theological reflection on the person and work of Christ, namely the restriction of Christology to Jesus's teaching and death and the failure to accord constitutive significance to his resurrection, ascension, and high priesthood, and hence to the working of the Holy Spirit. The casualty of this restriction is the presence of Christ. Jesus comes to be largely a silent, remote figure from the past who neither speaks nor acts now. As this absent figure, he does not turn to us or make himself present, leaving the space between him and us to be filled by tradition as a human undertaking, through which we make him contemporary. If we are to advance here, what is required above all is a theology of the presence of Christ. Such a theology will not invalidate tradition, but it will both circumscribe and redefine its role by setting it in the context of an understanding of Christ as the prophet of his own presence. I want to try to sketch such an account and then move on to trace some of its effects on our understanding of tradition as the "public covenant" of Christianity.

Jesus the risen one is our contemporary. He is alive and ascended; he sits at the right hand of God in the glory of the Father; he shares in the eternity of God. His existence, therefore, is not circumscribed or exhausted by his earthly manifestation in the days of his flesh, for that manifestation is the presence in time of what he eternally is. And so his historical existence is surrounded by his pre-existence and his post-existence. Because he is such a one, we have to say of him above all else: he *is*, and therefore he is here and now. He is the field within which all creaturely occurrence, including our own, takes place. Our time and space are what they are because in them he is present to us. We have already noted how, at the beginning of the Apocalypse, the glorified Jesus describes himself thus: "I am the first and the last, and the living one; I died, and behold, I am alive for evermore" (Rev. 1:17–18). What is, perhaps, most important in understanding that statement is the way in which it echoes the divine name in the same chapter of the Apocalypse: "Grace to you and peace from him who is and who was and who is to come" (v. 4), and "'I am the Alpha and the Omega,' says the Lord God, who is and who was and who is to come, the Almighty" (v. 8).

Jesus the risen one thus shares the eternity of God. This does not mean his *removal* from us but precisely the opposite: it means that he is with us, that he is our contemporary. In *Training in Christianity*, Kierkegaard writes thus of the contemporaneity of Christ:

> In relation to the absolute there is only one tense: the present. For him who is not a contemporary with the absolute—for him it has no existence. And as Christ is the absolute, it is easy to see that with respect to Him there is only one situation: that of contemporaneousness. The five, the seven, the fifteen, the eighteen hundred years are neither here nor there; they do not change Him, neither do they in any wise reveal who He was, for who He is is revealed only to faith. . . . Christ is . . . not at all a merely historical person. . . . What really occurred (the past) is not . . . the real. It lacks the determinant which is the determinant of truth (as inwardness) and of all religiousness, the *for thee*. The past is not reality—for me: only the contemporary is reality for me. What thou dost live contemporaneous with is reality—for thee. And thus every man can be contemporary only with the age in which he lives—and then with one thing more: with Christ's life on earth; for Christ's life on earth, sacred history, stands for itself alone outside history. . . . His earthly life accompanies the race, and accompanies every generation in particular, as the eternal history; His earthly life possesses the eternal contemporaneousness.[11]

11. Søren Kierkegaard, *Training in Christianity, and the Edifying Discourse Which "Accompanied" It* (Princeton: Princeton University Press, 1944), 67–68.

This is an extraordinarily instructive passage. Though not expressed in the formal language of dogmatics, Kierkegaard's point here is to secure the centrality of the presence of Christ for the condition of the Christian believer. "Christ is the absolute"; that is, he participates in the eternal presence of God to all time and all persons. This is why Kierkegaard says that "with respect to Him there is only one situation: that of contemporaneousness." And, moreover, this is why Kierkegaard is marvelously unimpressed by the so-called problem of historical distance between Christ and us. He simply states unequivocally that Jesus's "earthly life accompanies the race, and accompanies every generation in particular." This leads Kierkegaard to his strange statement that "what has really occurred (the past) is not . . . the real," since it lacks the element of "*for thee*." It would be possible to read Kierkegaard as advocating a purely subjective Christology, in which Jesus has no independence over against the believer but depends for his reality on our "realization" of him. But the entire drift of his thought here is in another direction: the "for me" is a function of his presence, not of the dynamics of my reception. If, nevertheless, Kierkegaard does not take us far enough, it is because he—in company with much Protestant dogmatics since the Reformation—has too slender a theology of the Holy Spirit. For it is above all to the doctrine of the Holy Spirit that one looks in order to describe how it is that Jesus turns to us, making himself present, and binding his life and ours together, so that the *extra nos* and the *in nobis* can be seen in their inseparability. "The Holy Spirit is the bond by which Christ effectually unites us to himself," says Calvin (arguably the first and last great Protestant theologian of the Spirit): "He unites us to himself by the Spirit alone."[12]

How do the Spirit-realized presence of Christ and tradition relate to each other? One well-tried way of stating the matter is to say that the tradition of the church is the historical embodiment of the presence of Christ in the Spirit. Tradition—the stream of life of the Christian community—is life in Christ, for through the Spirit Christ has so united himself to his church that it can be spoken of in densely realistic fashion as his body. Thus Joseph Ratzinger, for

12. John Calvin, *Institutes of the Christian Religion*, ed. John T. McNeill, trans. Ford Lewis Battles (Philadelphia: Westminster, 1960), III.i.1, at 538, and III.i.3, at 541.

example, writes of tradition as "an interpretation of the Christ-event itself on the basis of the *pneuma*, which means on the basis of the Church's present. The latter is possible because Christ is not dead but living, not only Christ yesterday but Christ today and tomorrow. But it is precisely in his Church that he is living and present; in the Church which is his Body in which his Spirit is active."[13] Or a modern Lutheran theologian, Robert Jenson, can write thus: "That the church is the body of Christ . . . means that the church is the object as which the risen Christ is available to be found, to be responded to, to be grasped. In the assembly of believers, where am I to direct my intention, in order to be intending my Lord? The first answer is: I am to look around me, at the assembly itself."[14] Appealing to the metaphor of the church as the body of Christ has the considerable advantage of enabling a frankly *theological* account of tradition: tradition is not mere natural process, but the historical embodiment of the risen Christ. But I have to confess to some Protestant (and, let it be said in hushed tones, Calvinist) discomfort with this account of the matter. This perspective on the life and tradition of the church rarely affords a sufficiently robust sense of the sheer unbridgeable difference between Christ and the church which, it is claimed, is his embodiment. Compacting Christ and the church too closely together, this perspective tends to neglect the sheer gratuity with which Christ declares the church to be flesh of his flesh, bone of his bone. (This is especially when, as in some recent versions, it makes appeal to the remarkably slippery notion of *koinōnia*.) Gift quickly becomes possession; the event of the Spirit's presentation of Christ and uniting of him to his body can be leveled into a steady state.

Such discomfort may, however, be eased, by making a shift of the idiom in which the relation between the present Christ and the "traditioned" life of the church is expressed. Rather than making *embodiment* the leading concept to formulate that relation, I suggest that priority be accorded to *apostolicity*. *Tradition is the apostolic*

13. Joseph Ratzinger, "Revelation and Tradition," in *Revelation and Tradition*, ed. Karl Rahner and Joseph Ratzinger (London: Burns & Oates, 1966), 25–49, at 42.

14. Robert W. Jenson, "The Church and the Sacraments," in *The Cambridge Companion to Christian Doctrine*, ed. Colin E. Gunton (Cambridge: Cambridge University Press, 1997), 205–27, at 210.

form of the life of the church. By way of expansion, several points may be made.

First, tradition is a definite, historical form of human life; it is, indeed, a "public covenant." It involves *tradita*, things handed on, the contents of tradition, as well as *traditio*, the acts and processes of transmission. Tradition is the human—political, social, cultural—*visibility* of the church: anything else is docetism. But this visibility is a "special visibility," involving more than simply the church's phenomenal form.[15] The visibility of the church "has this character in virtue of the reconciling and self-revealing grace of God, in virtue of the mission and work of the Holy Spirit, and therefore in the power of Jesus Christ himself."[16] The apostolic form of the life of the church is what it is because of the presence and activity of Jesus Christ, the one who ever afresh makes himself present and manifest in the event of the Spirit's coming. Such affirmations are a critical safeguard against the potential in the metaphor of the body of Christ to suggest an unqualified identification of the mystery of the church with its empirical or phenomenal visibility. Whatever else it may be, however much it may live "in Christ," the public covenant of the church is no second Christ, no extension or prolongation of his presence.

Second, therefore, the tradition, that is the form of life, of the church is apostolic because it is called and commissioned by Jesus Christ in the power of his Spirit. In speaking of calling and commissioning, we are not indicating something merely archaeological. That is, we are not simply identifying some originary vocation "in the beginning," or an initial impulse which sets the tradition in motion but after which it perpetuates itself. The calling and commissioning of Christ are the calling and commissioning of one who is our contemporary, constituting our present and not merely addressing it from the past. He summons his community now, and the summons is always fresh; we hear his voice, as Hebrews says, picking up Psalm 95, "today" (Heb. 3:15; 4:7).

Third, as the one who issues the call to be the apostolic community, Jesus Christ is the free Lord who himself generates that which he evokes. "Just as Jesus Christ is a free subject when it takes place

15. Karl Barth, *Church Dogmatics* IV/1 (Edinburgh: T&T Clark, 1956), 654.
16. Barth, *Church Dogmatics* IV/1, 656.

that the apostles become apostles, it is again an event in which Jesus
Christ is a free subject and His Spirit moves where He wills when the
apostolic community comes into being and exists as such."[17] Apostolicity is a matter of election. It therefore simply bypasses the issue
of human capacity. Natural giftedness or suitability simply does not
enter into the picture, because the calling of the apostolic community
is an appointment which brings into being that which it commissions.
Of this, the calling of the Twelve is paradigmatic in the sheer, intrusive authority of the divine call and in the immediacy of response
which that brings about.

All this serves to emphasize that the "public covenant" of the
church is the spiritual event of assembly around, and life from, the
summons of God in Christ through the Spirit. The apostolic community which is so constituted is given a definite task. This task is
that of witness. Witness is a second, not a first word. The witness-
ing task of the apostolic community is to indicate what Jesus Christ
himself has said and done and now says and does in the Spirit. The
community does not speak his word or perform his actions for him
as his substitute, the mouth of one who is no longer capable of utterance, or the body of one no longer able to act. He speaks and acts,
and the speech and acts of the community which assembles around
him in response to his calling and appointment have as their sole
task that of confession. Everything that is to be said of the church
is said by saying: "We point to him."[18] Proclamation, the celebration of the sacraments of the gospel, fellowship, mission, service,
theology—all of the things which make up the social and cultural
and political world of the apostolic community—are nothing other
than a gesture in which the church directs attention to Jesus's inexhaustibly prior reality. Because of this, therefore, tradition is "eschatological": its center is in the presence and activity of another, in
the event of the coming of Jesus Christ, and its primary activity is
the Spirit-produced activity of faith. Jesus Christ is with his church
because he is always "in coming," and his coming never transforms
itself into immanence within the statutory life of the apostolic public
covenant. For this reason, the Christian tradition is in one important

17. Barth, *Church Dogmatics* IV/1, 718.
18. Cf. Karl Barth, *Church Dogmatics* IV/3 (Edinburgh: T&T Clark, 1961), 797.

sense never "conservative." Certainly it has "locative" functions: it affords a sense of place, of order and value which is inherited rather than produced *ex nihilo* at each moment. But the "place" which it offers is such that at the same time it subverts, setting before us that which is simply not us and not ours.

⇒•⇐

Such, in short compass, is tradition as the apostolic way of life of the church. What is the task of theology in relation to this way of life?

Theology is one of the ways in which the Christian tradition inquires into its apostolic character. Theology is not an inquiry into the *possibility* of the Christian tradition. Its task, in other words, is not to construct *a priori* arguments to establish whether there can or cannot be such a thing as the Christian tradition. For Christian theology, the possibility of there being such a reality is given in the fact that there indeed is such a reality. In this sense, theology is a subsequent move, a reflection upon what has already been given in Jesus Christ and announced in the gospel. *Whether* there *is* a gospel is a question which has already been answered for theology; its task is to inquire into the relation of this given reality to the apostolic form of life which is called to indicate the gospel. Accordingly, theology's relation to the public covenant of the community of faith is complex, and not something that can be defined in terms of a single, invariant role or stance.

Theology has a descriptive or, we might say, didactic task. In this mode of operation, theology offers a loving, Christianly rich and persuasive depiction of the Christian good news, an orderly statement of an amazing reality. Theology is what Hans Frei once called, in a lovely phrase, "a praise of God by the use of the analytical capacities."[19] As such, he went on, "this exercise of ordering and of praise" is "an exercise in clarification"; it takes what is "already established" and offers nothing more than "a kind of descriptive expansion."[20] Such descriptive expansion is accomplished by offering what I earlier called "repetitions" of Holy Scripture, whose end is edification by promoting fidelity to the gospel which gives life.

19. Hans W. Frei, *The Identity of Jesus Christ: The Hermeneutical Bases of Dogmatic Theology* (Philadelphia: Fortress, 1975), 5.
20. Frei, *Identity*, 5.

But theology is also one of the ways in which the tradition of the church offers resistance to its own tendency to closure. It is thus a form of protest against transforming the revolution of the gospel into mere equilibrium. Such a transformation is an ever-present threat to the tradition of the church, because its apostolic character cannot be simply a material given but a spiritual event. When for whatever reason the phenomena of apostolicity—orders, doctrines, patterns of speech and action—somehow acquire relative detachment from the event of the coming of Christ in the Spirit, then apostolicity is as it were naturalized or routinized, and thereby the phenomena themselves come to take on quasi-absolute characteristics. What is the task of theology in this situation?

One of the most commonly canvassed responses to that question proposes that the critical task of theology is to de-absolutize the tradition by displaying it as a contingent set of historical acts of "negotiation," of processes of managing, assimilating, and transforming the materials of common life and culture. Delwin Brown, for instance, in his recent work *Boundaries of Our Habitations*, writes thus: "Tradition is cultural negotiation circumscribed by a canon, a more or less explicit field of play formed in history."[21] Like cultures, traditions are "processes of bartering and bargaining, sustaining and creating, establishing and subverting."[22] Viewed thus, as a sort of teeming bazaar in which an almost limitless variety of transactions can take place, traditions can certainly no longer present themselves with an unqualified claim upon our allegiance. Yet the price is clearly the scaling down of apostolicity; viewed solely from the human end, tradition may come to be described as mere human economy. And so the question presents itself: Are there theological resources to be brought to bear on the question of the ideological potential of tradition? Does theology have a responsibility beyond that of simply effecting the destabilizing of settled cultural forms?

At this point, appeal might be made to a number of doctrinal themes. One move—often made in postmodern theology of various kinds—is to underline the nonrepresentable nature of God. What

21. Brown, *Boundaries of Our Habitations*, 77
22. Brown, *Boundaries of Our Habitations*, 90.

is gained here is critical purchase against the excessive stability of settled traditional forms; but there is at least a question whether a severely apophatic doctrine of God is too high a price to pay. Another, more christologically specific, line of appeal points to the catholicity of Christ. As the risen one who shares in God's very life, Jesus Christ is limitlessly resourceful. No one rendering of him can exhaust his potential; no single schema of tradition can issue in a "final" statement of his identity in relation to human life and history, for he is literally infinite. However, such appeals do not take place apart from appeal to Holy Scripture. The tradition is opened to correction by attentiveness to the gospel, not by passing the gospel through the sieve of prior notions of the contingency of all representations. And attentiveness to the gospel always involves attention to Holy Scripture as the appointed testimony to the gospel.

Fulfilling the theological task in this way involves bearing in mind the dialectical relation of Scripture and tradition. Scripture is, of course, not without tradition. Its production, authorization, and reception are inescapably "traditional" activities, the acts of human agents within the larger social processes of which they form part. "Tradition" is in large part the accumulated store of the receptions, or readings, of Scripture by the church—not a passively inherited deposit but active assimilation, response, and "performance" of the constitutional text of Christian practice.[23] Yet Scripture does not thereby relinquish its "overagainstness" in its relation to tradition.[24] Scripture is canon, norm. As such, it may reconstruct and revise, and even overthrow, tradition, but it is not itself open to reconstruction, revision, or overthrow. Tradition is the canon's field of operation, but it is itself impermeable to tradition. Precisely because it is resistant to assimilation, Scripture is the instrument which prevents any de-eschatologizing of the Christian tradition—that is, any attempt to stifle or domesticate the relation of apostolic faith and practice to a

23. For the metaphor of "performance," see Nicholas Lash, "Performing the Scriptures," in *Theology on the Way to Emmaus* (London: SCM, 1986), 37–46, and, more recently, Frances Young, *The Art of Performance: Towards a Theology of Holy Scripture* (London: Darton, Longman & Todd, 1990).

24. Maurice Wiles, "The Uses of 'Holy Scripture,'" in *Explorations in Theology* 4 (London: SCM, 1979), 73–82, at 81.

final, absolute source beyond itself in Christ and Spirit. The task of theology is to watch, contribute to, and sometimes to intervene critically in the apostolic life of the church so that that life can be nothing other than what it already is: the public covenant of the gospel.

⟫⟫◆◇◆⟪⟪

Let me draw matters to a close. I've tried to argue that the relation of theology to the Christian tradition becomes clear when we understand that tradition as apostolic—that is, as a set of human readings of the gospel which, like everything else in the life of the church, is a space in which Jesus Christ announces and presents himself in the power of the Spirit as one who is indefatigably alive. The tradition of the church indicates this one—Jesus present—and theology assists the tradition in two ways: by exemplary indication and by countering the drift of the tradition into stasis or self-satisfaction. Good theology usually does both these jobs, though at any given time priority will be given to one or other of them. Deciding which task is the more urgent in any particular context is a matter of prudential judgment, based on a reading of the situation—properly informed by a vivid sense of the gospel, its delights and demands—and a clear understanding of the ends of the theological enterprise.

We have already had occasion to consider some words from Kierke-gaard. In closing we may mention a celebrated essay from near the end of his life, "Of the Difference between a Genius and an Apostle." "What, exactly, have the errors of exegesis and philosophy done in order to confuse Christianity?" Kierkegaard asks.[25] His answer is that "paradox-religion" (what I've called the eschatological gospel) has been forced "into the sphere of aesthetics," and apostleship has been fatally confused with mere natural religious genius. "If the sphere of paradox-religion is abolished, or explained away in aesthetics, an Apostle becomes neither more nor less than a genius, and then—good night, Christianity."[26] "A genius and an apostle," he continues, "are qualitatively different, they are definitions which

25. Søren Kierkegaard, "Of the Difference between a Genius and an Apostle," in *The Present Age and Two Minor Ethico-Religious Treatises* (London: Oxford University Press, 1940), 139.

26. Kierkegaard, "Of the Difference," 139.

each belong in their own spheres: *the sphere of immanence and the sphere of transcendence.*[27] Genius is born: "it is a natural qualification," whereas "an Apostle is a man called and appointed by God."[28] The Christian tradition, I believe, is apostolic; but it is always threatened—as Kierkegaard saw with singular acuteness and distress—with becoming mere genius. Not the least of the undertakings of theology in the church is to set before the tradition its calling and appointment, and thereby to foster Christian difference.

27. Kierkegaard, "Of the Difference," 141.
28. Kierkegaard, "Of the Difference," 142–43.

4

Conversations

Engaging Difference

THE PROPOSAL WHICH I HAVE SO FAR MADE about the culture of theology may seem to make it into a rather exotic affair. This impression may be given in part because my suggestions about what theology ought to be don't bear all that much resemblance to the kinds of things that actually go on in research and teaching in biblical, doctrinal, and historical studies. But it's also something to do with the fact that my insistence throughout the argument on the fundamentally eschatological character of Christian faith and theology—no doubt, too strident an insistence for the taste of many—may give rise to the anxiety that theological reflection on this kind of faith could *in principle* never find any kind of place in the real world of scholarly activity. To map Christian faith and its reflective practices in a thoroughly eschatological projection may make theology "exotic" in the sense of never having a home in any stable set of practices, let alone in any regular institution. If, as I suggested earlier, an eschatological faith always stands under the sign of its own contradiction, can a theology governed by such a faith be anything other than literally outlandish, never to be naturalized or acclimatized, and therefore, in short, an impossibility?

If you have worries along those lines, I share them, and I want to try and address them in the three lectures which follow. I want to give some attention to the question of the forms which the intellectual task of theology might assume. In this lecture, I want to think a little about the sort of institution in which the style of theology which I'm recommending might be practiced; in particular, I'll be concerned with the place of theology in the university. In the next lecture, I want us to turn our attention to the more specific question of what is involved in the practice of *critical* theology. And in the last lecture, I want to try and offer an idealized portrait of the kind of person which the theologian is required to be if he or she is to do the task well. In sum, what I hope to cover is a politics, a critical theory, and an ethics of the theological task.

I ought to say at the outset that, for those among you who are hard-nosed realists, wanting to know how my account of the nature and tasks of theology can be translated into something specific enough to be delivered as a theological curriculum, I haven't got a great deal on offer. There are certainly curricular consequences in what I have to say: most obvious among these, for example, is something mentioned in an earlier lecture, namely the need for a drastic reordering of the curriculum so that close to its center is a certain manner of reading the classics of the Christian tradition. But rather than focus on these issues here, important as they are, I want to offer something which is essentially utopian and which does not conform to any institution I know. I fear that this will mean that some of you will judge that we are still in the eschatological stratosphere, and confirm you in your view that that appeal to eschatology in matters of educational practice is irresponsible. But it's worth reflecting that the real aim of utopias is not to give free rein to fantasy and certainly not to flee from assuming responsibility for the places and institutional structures where we find ourselves. Utopias afford us a vantage point from which we can see our present as it is in its relativity and contingency and from which we can therefore begin to consider the possibility that things could be other than they are. So the sketch which follows is not in any sense a blueprint but a sort of horizon, by looking to which we may be stimulated to ask about the sorts of local practices which might approximate to the ideal.

What, then, of Christian theology in the university? It's important at the beginning to secure the point that there is no necessary connection of theology to the university as it has developed since the early nineteenth century. (The founding of the University of Berlin usually serves as the convenient marker for the beginnings of the modern academy.) Indeed, it would be possible to argue that the ethos of the modern secular research university is such that Christian theology can only exist there at cost to some of its positive character as the reflective life of the culture of faith.

It is, I believe, beyond dispute that theology's place in the university has often been bought at the price of a measure of assimilation of some of the theological subdisciplines to the procedures of neighboring nontheological disciplines (biblical studies to history of religions, doctrine to philosophy, and so forth), as it were knocking off the rough edges of theology in order to make it a respectable undertaking in the universe of scholarship as currently established. When this takes place, then in effect the matter of theology is trimmed or adjusted, with greater or lesser degrees of cooperation or protest, to effect conformity to the demands of a culture of scholarship and rational practice which defines itself, in part at least, in terms of exclusion of such merely domestic concerns as Christian teaching. The history, of course, is highly complex and cannot be captured in a few slogans; theologians have struck all sorts of local deals with universities and built up nearer or more distant relationships of various kinds, with varying degrees of pressure brought to bear on theological activity by the host institution to bring its procedures and subject matter into line. Theologians who have valued these relationships enough to work at fostering them have done so from a range of motives—sometimes simply bad scholarly conscience about the viability of Christian theology, sometimes a genuine desire to retain something of the public character of theology as a full contributor to the discourses of higher learning, sometimes an anxiety that a theology whose audience is simply the ecclesial community may become dangerously introverted and fail to sustain serious engagements with what lies outside. Others have been less impressed by the gains of such relationships and more regretful of the losses and accordingly have chosen to undertake theology elsewhere. Clearly, there is no principled answer to the question of Christian theology's place in the university; everything hangs on what you mean by "Christian theology," "university," and, of course, "in."

When we ask about the dynamics of the pursuit of Christian theology in the university, we often fall into the trap of phrasing the question in the wrong way, that is, in a way which assumes that the university as it has developed in modernity embodies ideals of intellectual practice to which all modes of discourse which seek to engage in public debate must conform. I want to look at things from a different angle. Rather than starting by asking the question, "What sort of discipline does Christian theology need to be if it is to be accorded a place in the public academy?" I propose that we should begin by asking, "What sort of institution might the academy have to become if it is to profit from having Christian theology as a contributor to its conversations?"

My answer to the question runs something like this: If the kind of theology which I have been recommending in these lectures is to be undertaken in institutions of higher learning, then what is needed more than anything else is a better politics of intellectual exchange. In particular, we need to learn what might be involved in conducting the intellectual affairs of the university as a "conflict" (or, perhaps better, a "conversation") of the faculties. By this, I mean a good deal more than the sort of interdisciplinary encounter in which we inform ourselves in an untroubled way about what people in other departments are doing and then go back to our own corner (though in modern universities, where disciplinary demarcations tend to be quite sharp, even within the humanities, that itself is no mean achievement).

The conflict or conversation I have in mind as the heart of the university's business is more fundamental than comparing notes with cognate scholars. It is an exchange which is a contest, involving argument about fundamental claims about human life, including fundamental claims about the life of the mind. Membership of a community of inquiry whose basic end is argument about *difference* is thus consent to conflict. The conditions required for such a contest to take place effectively are manifold. Not the least among them are economic and administrative conditions—and the fulfillment of these conditions in late democratic societies usually involves the bruising business of negotiating some degree of distinctiveness from the wider society upon which the university remains nevertheless dependent and to whose welfare it continues to believe itself to be a contributor. But there are also conditions which are more internal to the way in which academic communities conduct their practices of learning: political, rhetorical, and ethical conditions. That is, the pursuit of the goal of conversational conflict requires a certain politics of intellectual relations; it requires certain strategies of communicative action; and it requires that the participants in the dispute strive to acquire, exercise, and refine certain virtues.

Though these kinds of contests do take place in universities, there is much about dominant models of scholarship which nevertheless serves to inhibit such exchange or restrict the range of its participants. The rather insecure place of Christian theology (especially of Christian theology, which claims much by way of distinctiveness in content and procedure) in the university is but one example of a more general inhospitality to discourse generated by socially marginal communities with strong moral, political, or religious concerns: feminism and Marxist theory being other obvious examples. My suggestion is that the real contribution of Christian theology to the university will not be made by suspending its strong concerns; even less will it be by transforming itself into a purveyor of so-called values (a deadly role which almost always ensures the reduction of theology to silence on crucial matters of substance). Its contribution will be *nonconformity*: an unanxious pursuit of its own proper concerns, which goes hand in hand with a resistance to calling too early a truce in the conflict of the faculties or to calling the wrong kind of truce. The extraordinarily high level of anxiety which has often been shown by theology about its place in the universe of learning, its deference to more prestigious models of inquiry, and its reticence in fielding its own rhetoric or appealing to its own grounds—all these defensive gestures are unnecessary once theology ceases to rely on a policy of compliance and instead makes its contribution to the conversation of the faculties by being nothing other than itself. In brief: what Christian theology has to say is what Heidegger (in a magisterial 1927 lecture on the relation of theology and philosophy) summed up in a single word: "Christianness."[1]

———◆◇◆———

Before talking a little about the way in which this affects our conception of the theological task, we need to ask a prior question: What is involved in envisaging the university as a matter of conversational conflict between the faculties? Two contrasts may help make the point.

First, to speak of the university as involving a contest of the faculties is not to think of the university as presided over by the tribunal of reason. In his re-examination of Newman's *Idea of the University*, Jaroslav Pelikan proposes that "the university is, in God's good world, the principal community through which human rationality can examine all existing communities."[2] This model—the university as a place where all particular, local claims are brought before reason as before a judgment seat, there to have their rationality adjudicated—has undergone sustained political and moral criticism in the last couple of decades, but it is worth reminding ourselves of some of its weaknesses, precisely because, despite the criticism, it remains a model with massive institutional presence. Most obviously, it is a model which seriously neglects the constitutive role played by tradition in intellectual life, especially in the formulation and application of criteria of excellence in inquiry. It is, indeed, an extension to the field of intellectual inquiry of a forensic ideal of blind judgment, one which therefore excludes particular interests and their rhetorics as always antithetical to right judgment in matters of reason. For all the universality to which this aspires, it remains in itself a local anthropology and politics of the intellect. Indeed, thinking of the university in this way tends to prioritize certain disciplines which more easily associate themselves with the tribunal model of the university. Again, the cogency of the model depends less on its self-evident universality and

1. Martin Heidegger, "Phenomenology and Theology," in *The Piety of Thinking: Essays by Martin Heidegger*, ed. James G. Hart and John C. Maraldo (Bloomington: Indiana University Press, 1976), 5–21, at 9–10.

2. Jaroslav Pelikan, *The Idea of the University: A Re-examination* (New Haven: Yale University Press, 1992), 67.

more on the social prestige of some of the disciplines which embody it: natural science, medicine, and some styles of philosophy, social science, and perhaps history.

At most we can say that this model catches only one operation of the university; but when that operation is totalized, then a number of disciplines are pushed to the margins. This is not merely because they cannot aspire to its ideals but more because the very practice of such disciplines in the academy gives expression to critical reservations about those ideals and about the politics and anthropology which undergird them. Thus Christian theology, at least in some of its versions, will be deeply uneasy with any account of intellectual life in which the judging function of reason has central place. Above all, this is because the habits of mind, the intellectual temper, which have their center in the act of judgment, are hard to reconcile with some primary affirmations of Christian anthropology—for example, with affirmations that human life is properly a matter of answerability or of response to the disorientation brought about by a challenge, and therefore that attention and faith are more humanly and Christianly basic than representation and judgment. Put differently, we might want to say that for Christian faith, truth is not primarily to be identified with a judgment made by us but with our interception and remaking. "As the interruption of the cohesion of the world, [truth] brings that world into . . . a light which makes everything appear in a new light."[3] Thinking is "truthful" insofar as it is engendered by the invasion of the world, its being broken apart by the presence of that which is unconditional, an *origin* of all things which is not itself judged but which judges all things. As Barth put it in his lectures on ethics from the later 1920s, intellectual reflection is itself interrogated by "the question of origin," by what he called "the question of truth in truth, of superior, unconditional truth," which "is understood as the question that is primarily put by the *object* to us." He went on,

> We see it as the question of the origin that precedes all being when we see it as being prior in order to the questions of our general and

3. Eberhard Jüngel, "Invocation of God as the Ethical Ground of Christian Action," in *Theological Essays I*, ed. J. B. Webster (Edinburgh: T&T Clark, 1989), 154–72, at 172.

theoretical thinking . . . as the question which we *cannot* answer inci-
dentally from the safe harbour of our self-consciousness as spectators
of our own life, but which we can, indeed, whether we like it or not,
we *must* answer only with our life itself, to which our whole active
life and each of our individual acts . . . *must* be viewed as the answer,
in relation to which our whole existence takes on the character of
answerability.[4]

Viewed in this light, there is something disabling, even corrupt, about
regarding the intellectual life and its institutions as simply places of
judgment, and one of the most important contributions to be made
by Christian theology is the promotion of critical debate about this
ideal and the exemplification of strong alternatives.

A briefer, second contrast may be drawn at this point. To talk of
the university as, at heart, a contest of the faculties is not simply to
envisage it as a free market of opinion in which divergent intellectual
cultures co-exist but never engage in any fundamental conflict. The
deficiencies of this kind of perspectivalism have, once again, been re-
hearsed in critical reception of postmodernism. It is potentially conservative in that it rarely mounts a serious challenge to whatever happens
to have achieved cultural dominance. Its fundamentally ironic stance
runs the risk of trivializing the claims made by specific traditions, rendering them matters of play rather than of argument seeking to establish allegiance. It may encourage infinite deferral of decision-making.
It is not easy to extricate it from the dynamics of consumption. For
all this, at first glance the frank pluralism of this model appears much
more hospitable to the difference which Christian theology represents;
yet the price is that Christian theology becomes little more than one
more source of amusement, one more item for curiosity. Moreover,
Christian theology has some serious doctrinal reserves here, most of
all, again, with the underlying anthropology, which is hard to reconcile
with Christian affirmations. It is an anthropology whose core is *desire*.[5]
And thereby it promotes a disposition which is antithetical to that

4. Karl Barth, *Ethics* (Edinburgh: T&T Clark, 1981), 65–66; cf. Thomas F. Torrance, "Questioning in Christ," in *Theology in Reconstruction* (London: SCM, 1965),
117–27.
5. See here Roger Lundin, *The Culture of Interpretation: Christian Faith and the
Postmodern World* (Grand Rapids: Eerdmans, 1993), 31–52.

which is required for the prosecution of serious Christian theology, the baptismal pattern which emerges from the gospel's announcement of judgment and grace, repentance and faith.

To sum up so far: when we reflect on the nature and purposes of institutions of higher learning, we often find ourselves caught between the primacy of technical or forensic reason on the one hand and the infinite play of desire on the other. Indeed, instrumentalism and the free play of the mind are in important ways mirror images of each other: one is the technics of human autonomy, the other its aesthetics. Neither can make much sense of the university as a place for *positive sciences*, that is, for the intellectual self-articulations of particular, interested visions of human life and flourishing. Lacking the capacity to mark out a space in which such positive sciences can collide and engage in mutual conversation, both these models of the university in the end serve to inhibit growth and change by failing to promote encounter with "authentic otherness."[6] Richard Rorty—often but not wholly justifiably targeted as the promoter of pure perspectivalism—once wrote,

No description of how things are from a God's eye point of view, no skyhook provided by some contemporary or yet-to-be-developed science, is going to free us from the contingency of having been acculturated as we were. . . . We can only hope to transcend our acculturation if our culture contains (or, thanks to disruptions from outside or internal revolt, comes to contain) splits which supply toeholds for new initiatives. Without such splits—without tensions which make people listen to unfamiliar ideas in the hope of finding means of overcoming those tensions—there is no such hope. . . . So our best chance for transcending our acculturation is to be brought up in a culture which prides itself on not being monolithic—on its tolerance for a plurality of subcultures and its willingness to listen to neighbouring cultures.[7]

6. George Parkin Grant, "Faith and Multiversity," in *Technology and Justice* (Notre Dame, IN: University of Notre Dame Press, 1986), 35–77, at 38; see also Nita Graham, "Teaching against the Spirit of the Age: George Grant and the Museum Culture," in *George Grant and the Subversion of Modernity*, ed. Arthur Davis (Toronto: University of Toronto Press, 1996), 285–303.

7. Richard Rorty, "Introduction: Antirepresentationalism, Ethnocentrism, and Liberalism," in *Objectivity, Relativism, and Truth: Philosophical Papers*, vol. 1 (Cambridge: Cambridge University Press, 1991), 1–17, at 13–14.

Universities, I suggest, are institutions which ought systematically to
hunt out and enlarge such "splits" and enable us to "climb outside"
of our own minds."[8] One of the things that happens in the contest
of the faculties is such a hunt for "splits," and part of the significance of Christian theology for the university (and of the university
for Christian theology) is that of being a place which registers the
shock of the new.

How does this contest of the faculties proceed? What sort of politics of intellectual exchange is required here?

First, the university may be envisaged as a *collegium* of positive
sciences, each with distinctive (if overlapping) contents and modes of
inquiry, which require of their practitioners different habits of mind.
Realizing such an ideal means relinquishing the ideal that learning is a
"generically human enterprise," humanly basic and—like freedom—
unaffected and unformed by circumstance and locality. Learning is
"the subject of contest."[9] And relinquishing the idea that it isn't
means bringing to explicit awareness the conventions about the nature of learning which operate in various institutional settings, and
especially the contests about such conventions which the *collegium*
contains but which are often kept from our view by the prestige of
one or other convention which has acquired normative status. Such
"bringing to awareness" is itself not merely an innocent matter of
putting information into the domain of public debate in the academy.
It involves a struggle against conventions and therefore is an inher-
ently political task. Accordingly, one of the primary conditions for
the advancement of the academy's contents is openness to difference,
not as mere unfocused celebration of formless plurality, but as the
imperative consequence of the fact that the university is the place
where different positive sciences are set in relation.

In this *collegium* of positive sciences, different spheres of intellectual inquiry relate by *colloquy*, that is, by energetic, committed attempts to describe to others the different *posita* which are

8. Thomas Nagel, *The View from Nowhere* (Oxford: Oxford University Press,
1986), 11.

9. Nicholas Wolterstorff, "The Travail of Theology in the Modern Academy," in
The Future of Theology: Essays in Honour of Jürgen Moltmann, ed. Miroslav Volf,
Carmen Krieg, and Thomas Kucharz (Grand Rapids: Eerdmans, 1996), 35–46, at 38.

foundational to their respective spheres and which find expression in distinctive disciplinary arrangements, subject matters, and modes of inquiry. It is this process—of explicating one positive discipline to another and attending to the self-explications of others—that is indicated by the term "conversation" in my title. The use of the metaphor of conversation to depict the life of the mind has become virtually banal, but it has nevertheless proved invaluable, both in helping us attain critical purchase against the hegemony of certain rationalist procedures and in alerting us to modes of discourse in premodern texts which do not naturally conform to the monological norms of some standard modern styles of argument.[10] The metaphor was famously used by Michael Oakeshott in a quietly revolutionary article on the nature of intellectual inquiry. He wrote, "The view dies hard that Babel was the occasion of a curse being laid upon mankind from which it is the business of philosophers to deliver us, and a disposition remains to impose a single character upon human speech."[11]

Oakeshott identifies something to which we have returned on a number of occasions in these lectures, namely the profoundly incapacitating effect of the flight from the local. In protesting against such flight, he speaks of conversation between different idioms as "an unrehearsed intellectual adventure" in which "different universes of discourse meet, acknowledge each other and enjoy an oblique relationship which neither requires nor forecasts their being assimilated to one another."[12] If Oakeshott is right, then conversation in the *collegium* of the university is not a matter of one of the positive sciences putting forward a claim to be the foundation of all others: certainly not theology as the queen of the sciences, nor, perhaps, analytic philosophy or natural science as some kind of knavish usurpers to the throne. The simple reason for this is that no science can claim to be

10. See here Quentin Skinner, *Reason and Rhetoric in the Philosophy of Hobbes* (Cambridge: Cambridge University Press, 1996); Hans-Georg Gadamer, *Truth and Method* (London: Sheed & Ward, 1979), 325–33; David Tracy, *The Analogical Imagination: Christian Theology and the Culture of Pluralism* (London: SCM, 1981), and *Plurality and Ambiguity: Hermeneutics, Religion, Hope* (San Francisco: Harper & Row, 1987).

11. Michael Oakeshott, *The Voice of Poetry in the Conversation of Mankind: An Essay* (London: Bowes & Bowes, 1959), 9.

12. Oakeshott, *Voice of Poetry*, 11.

nonstatutory, nonlocal, "critical" *rather than* "positive"; no single science can embody universality. Nor is the aim of conversation in the *collegium* to sponsor the kind of encounter between different positive sciences whose result is that one or other of the participants is nudged, cajoled, or otherwise enticed to abandon its positive character. Indeed, one might say that a discipline which could so easily be dislodged in the course of intellectual exchange is one which already stands in an insecure relation to its own positivity—and one would not need to go too far to find theological illustrations of the problem.

What the contest or conversation of the faculties does require of its participants is *advocacy* and *attention*. "Advocacy" here means a kind of descriptive apologetic, that is, an *apologia pro se* which seeks to set forward a particular field of inquiry for consideration by giving the best, most imaginatively strenuous, rich, and dense depiction possible of its content and ways of proceeding. The terms for such a depiction will be derived, not from supposed commonplaces shared with other spheres of inquiry which will facilitate the task of explication, but from the cultural region to which this inquiry belongs and from which it takes its substance; hence such advocacy clearly depends upon prior immersion in that cultural region. In theological terms, this means that exegesis and dogmatics (along with symbolics and liturgics) precede apologetics; loving inhabitation of the specific region of faith and its practices is the prerequisite of addressing what is different. "Attention" means that each positive science will direct itself to what is said by the others in the conversation with a certain openness, almost naivete, which is the opposite of self-assurance and which, as Gadamer once put it, "distinguishes the experienced person from the person captivated by dogma."[13]

Why converse? Not in order to validate ourselves or others, nor to see how nearly we or others approximate some proposed absolute ideal of rationality, but in order to promote self-knowledge and self-critique through curious engagement with what is foreign to my space.

> The contention between different approaches, the traffic from different roads, has significant value. It exposes strengths and weaknesses of different contributions; it sharpens self-critical effort on the part of

13. Gadamer, *Truth and Method*, 325, English translation altered.

the participants. . . . The aspiration is not for the establishment of a
leader of the disciplines in a university, for a theory of everything. . . .
One does not expect contributors to resign from their fields, or even
necessarily to radically modify their approaches. . . . Rather, informed
and vigorous interaction that can be mutually edifying intellectually
is . . . what makes an institution approximate its traditional name,
"university."[14]

That being said, it is important not to be too sanguine about the ease
with which such ideals can find institutional expression. This kind
of colloquy of positive sciences has been and continues to be a rare
bird. One major inhibiting factor is the persistence with which some
disciplines dominate the conversation. Oakeshott notes that "in some
of the voices there are innate tendencies towards barbarism which
make it difficult to sustain," since "each voice is prone to *superbia*,
that is, an excessive concern with its own utterance, which may result in its identifying the conversation with itself and its speaking
as if it were speaking only to itself."[15] The kinds of skills in dialectic and questioning which this demands (so gracefully and lovingly
described in Gadamer's accounts of the Platonic dialogues) are not
easily learned, and the rhetoric of much academic argument tends
to inhibit rather than encourage their acquisition. One consequence
of "the suppression of questions by the dominant opinion"[16] is that
less powerful disciplines are tempted to ensure some sort of survival
for themselves by assimilating their practices or even their fields of
inquiry to those of the "master" disciplines. And so, for example,
while it would be quite unjust to claim that all religious studies are
theology *manqué*, the shift from positive theology to a certain kind
of study of religion makes study of Christianity much more companionable to the dominance of expressive individualism than does
the theology of Christian (or Buddhist or Islamic) difference. Yet the
price paid for such assimilation is often the downplaying of the particulars which make conversation both demanding and rewarding for

14. James M. Gustafson, *Intersections: Science, Theology, and Ethics* (Cleveland:
Pilgrim, 1996), xiii–xiv.
15. Oakeshott, *Voice of Poetry*, 12–13.
16. Gadamer, *Truth and Method*, 330.

participants. At its worst, conversation can descend into pure irony in
which genuine contests are simply dodged. As Stanley Hauerwas puts
it (with characteristic asperity), "Most universities find themselves
peculiarly ill-prepared to entertain such challenges since the university
serves the wider liberal polity through the suppression of conflict.
Universities, of course, pride themselves on 'freedom of speech,' as
well as on providing a 'safe' place for 'radical opinions,' but that is
exactly how conflict is domesticated. Namely, you can think and say
anything you wish as long as you accept the presumption that you
do not expect anyone to take you seriously."[17]

The presence of these threats to conversation serves to underline
that what is needed to promote real engagement across different fields
of inquiry is not a better epistemology, an even more universal foundational theory, or an ethic of limitless tolerance but a better politics
of intellectual conflict and a deeper and more self-aware inhabitation
of specific moral and intellectual cultures. And these threats ought
also to alert Christian theology to the need for a better *spirituality*
of intellectual exchange, that is, a better grasp of the spiritual conditions for genuine conversation. For Christian theology, conversation is
not a natural capacity and requires skills—of attentiveness, humility,
courage, and wit—which are graces. We do not by nature desire to
know, and coming to know is therefore a struggle to be educated.

> Education means that our natural development and activity are inter-
> sected. . . . Education means that someone wants more or less skillfully
> to take from me one of the many horns that I invisibly carry on my
> forehead, and of which I am as proud as a stag, and to put some kind of
> strange hat in its place. . . . I am supposed to wrestle with truths that did
> not grow in my own garden and for which I do not think I can find any
> place there. . . . The vile Thou of the educator is always there to tell me
> very simply from a loathsome position of superior strength that I must.[18]

Overdrawn, perhaps: but the Christian theologian has more reason
than anyone to be alert to the note of *superbia* in his or her own voice

---

17. Stanley Hauerwas, "Positioning: In the Church and University, but Not of
Either," in *Dispatches from the Front: Theological Engagements with the Secular*
(Durham, NC: Duke University Press, 1994), 5–28, at 13.
18. Barth, *Ethics*, 365.

and to know how hard it is to eradicate it. What does all this mean for the inhabitants of the eschatological culture of Christian faith?

⇒—◇—⇐

Christian theology will make its greatest contribution to the conversations of the academy when it pursues Christian difference with an easy conscience and with a measure of determination and doggedness in the face of those who would persuade it to do otherwise. Like Noah, Ezra, and Nehemiah, Christian theologians are to get on with the job without troubling themselves too much about the dissuaders. There is never a point at which Christian theology can absolve itself from the task of articulating its own world. It may never, for example, think that the internal, descriptive tasks have already been sufficiently attended to and can be laid aside for a while to pursue some opportunities for extramural work. There is no such thing as theological capital; the tasks of exegesis and dogmatics are never finished, even temporarily. When they cease to be matters of present activity and become simply an inheritance hovering in the background, then all too quickly Christian theology falls into the kind of confused or incoherent grasp of its proper subject matter, which not only weakens Christian identity but also robs it of anything pungent to say in the wider academy.

If the theologian really wants to be a theologian, then he or she "cannot wander at large among all other kinds of subjects,"[19] because to do so is to undermine the presence of the *positum* which is the theologian's concern. The theologian "cannot abstract away from this object. He cannot act as though God had not spoken, or perhaps had not spoken, or as though it had first to be investigated whether he had really done so."[20] As a rule, therefore, the more confident theology is in its own native habits of thought and speech, the more savory will be its contribution to the world of higher learning. Conversely, the periods when theology has been able to offer least resistance to its cultured despisers have been those marked by exegetical and dogmatic laziness, vacuity, or timidity.

19. Barth, *Ethics*, 40.
20. Barth, *Ethics*, 40.

But again: the pursuit of Christian difference is no straightforward business. There is a great deal to learn, much of it now not at all easy of access. And the process of learning itself is utterly demanding. It sets before us the devastating imperative of holiness, the transformation which is so basic to living the apostolic life. As we shall see in a later lecture, sanctification leaves nothing intact; there is little that is comfortable about the new creation. Yet without participation in the passion of regeneration, the theologian will be less than likely to have much to report when it is his or her turn to speak up in the colloquy of the sciences.

How might Christian theology profit from this kind of exchange? One of the persistent themes of these lectures has been that there is never a complete match between the gospel and any particular strand of Christian culture. No single form of Christian thought and witness can ever be a fully achieved rendering of its origin, which is a spiritual event and not a bit of religious property. Consequently, for all that Christian life and thought are ostensive, stretching out to indicate the gospel which brings them into being, they are still fabrications, things made by us. Theology can never fully close the gap between itself and its *positum*, the eschatological Word of God. Acknowledging this gap need not lead to some kind of precept of apophaticism. Such precepts rather readily cast Christian theology into a role dominated by self-subversion and can easily cancel the truly apostolic vocation of Christian thought and speech. What is required is rather that the discontinuity between the gospel and its representations should be seen as a space in which the critical task of theology is undertaken. The task of theological criticism is to inquire into the conformity of Christian witness to the given reality of the gospel. Though, as we shall see in the next lecture, the fundamental way in which theology achieves critical purchase on Christian witness is through appeal to the self-manifestation of Jesus present in the Spirit, the conversations of the academy—provided that they are not simply the monologue of instrumental reason or the free play of signs—are of no mean significance.

5

Criticism

Revelation and Disturbance

IS THE CULTURE OF CHRISTIAN FAITH capable of functioning as a self-critical culture? That is to say, is there an intrinsic connection between the inner contents of Christian teaching, on the one hand, and self-critical practices, on the other? I want in this lecture to answer those questions in the affirmative; further, I want to try and demonstrate that one of the tasks which Christian theology performs in the cultural space within which it operates is to participate in the church's critical self-evaluation. To make the argument, I want to draw attention to some of the salient features of the structure of Christian belief, above all to the doctrine of revelation. That doctrine, I shall argue, is in part concerned with identifying the grounds on which the Christian tradition may interrogate, evaluate, or even repudiate certain aspects of its development.

From the outset, it needs to be admitted that the argument seems counterintuitive. Almost by cultural instinct, we probably want to say that a culture of the eschatological kind which I have been portraying is the very antithesis of a self-critical form of life and thought. I have argued that the reflective practices of Christian faith are what we might in old-fashioned terms call a "civil theology," that is, they cannot be separated from the religious ways of a specific community. The force of the rationalist traditions of modernity has been to urge that there can be no connection between the contents of such a civil theology and the activities of criticism, precisely because criticism, properly understood, is inquiry into the conditions of possibility of particular ways of life and belief structures. Only as criticism transcends the dogmas of civil theologies can its work proceed responsibly and unhindered by prejudice. Most of what I want to say in this lecture is an attempt to undermine the instincts which lead us to polarize criticism and civil traditions. Those instincts cannot, however, be undermined simply by presenting a *theory* about criticism. Although along the way I want to risk a few general remarks about the nature of criticism, I do not consider any large-scale critical theory to be of much use unless we realize that criticism is essentially something specific to distinctive traditions and sets of social and cultural practices. Criticism with a capital C doesn't really exist, and those who promote the idea that it does tend to be imperialists, taking over bits of territory not their own and imposing the rule of foreign law, without taking account of the way in which indigenous peoples already do things. Rather than offering an overall theory of criticism, then, my intention is much more low-level: to look at the domestic culture of Christian faith and to try and observe the sorts of self-critical practices that go on there. The question, therefore, is not "What is criticism?" but "What is criticism *here*?"

The answer I want to try to offer to the question goes something like this: Christian faith and practice are always accompanied by self-criticism. As Christian culture goes about its business, and especially as it relates all its activities to the bewildering good news of the presence of God in judgment and mercy, it is always faced with the reality of the *distance* between itself and its ultimate source. That distance, I want to suggest, is what makes Christian culture a critical rather than simply a custom-bound culture. It is a culture whose fundamental impulse *subverts* as well as *grounds* the cultural activities which appeal to it. This point, which is quite fundamental for grasping the eschatological culture of Christian faith, could be traced by following virtually any major doctrinal trajectory in Christianity. To give merely one example, one might reflect that the so-called marks of the church are not simply bits of ecclesial self-inflation, claiming quasi-divine attributes for an all-too-human institution (unity?! holiness?!). Much more are they criteria by which that all-too-human institution can come to reflective awareness of the gulf between its divine commission and its actual practice and thereby be confronted with the need for repentance. Consideration of the content of Christian beliefs, that is, ought to lead us to the realization that relentless criticism is not only a requirement imposed from outside on an otherwise self-satisfied and recalcitrant community but also something primary to that community's vocation. The doctrinal area through which I want to trace this theme today is the doctrine of revelation, for it is one of the functions of Christian beliefs about revelation to engender and direct self-critical practice, doing so in the name of the transcendence of the God of the gospel.

There are two possible ways in which to construct an argument for the critical function of Christian claims about the revelatory action of God. The first starts from the general and works toward the particular. That is to say, it offers a phenomenology of revelation. It looks at the role which revelatory experience plays in human life and history, including, of course, religious life and history, and with the results it develops a theory of revelatory criticism which is then applied to the Christian tradition. The second starts from the particular and tends not to move too far from there. That is, it restricts itself to trying to map out the functions of appeal to revelation in the civil theology of the Christian church. It will come as no surprise that someone as theologically antediluvian as I am takes the latter route, but a glance at why I choose not to follow the former will nevertheless be worthwhile.

The task of the first way (a general theory of revelation rather than a theory of general revelation) would be to lay out the ways in which religious traditions are not simply conservative but, rather, contain resources which enable the critique of existing states of affairs; one such major resource is the notion of revelation. One could observe, for example, that the weakness of structural theories of religion is that they are insufficiently alert to the interplay of establishment and innovation which characterizes some religious traditions.[1] One could suggest that religion is not merely an accommodating or "stabilizing institution" but rather a means of opposing human life with a proposal about what it might become, a proposal which therefore performs critical functions.[2] One could certainly argue that those religious traditions which are imbued with a sense of the transcendent, nondegradable character of the divine have greater critical purchase against the fusion of ultimate reality and the orders of society.[3] And out of this, one might develop a phenomenology of religious (and possibly moral or aesthetic) life in which revelation is the intrusive presence of "possibility." Revelation, that is, might be envisaged as the gift of an order of being which is not neatly coextensive with what already is, whose surprising presence enables the censure and revision of human meaning in the light of the donation of something new.[4]

All this may certainly establish to our satisfaction that "the world is a revelatory kind of place"[5] and that religions are a source for critical human self-appraisal. It may even take us to the threshold of some of the things which Christian dogmatics will feel required to say. But Christian dogmatics does not simply take up the results of a general phenomenology of the religious, using it as a framework for the exposition of Christian teaching. Christian dogmatics is from the beginning a positive, not a comparative, exercise. It is singular and retrospective; its task is the limited one of reflection upon the *positum* of Christian faith. It is interested in *this*, in *here*. And furthermore, Christian dogmatics of this sort will be worried that a comparative rather than a positive account of revelation always runs the risk of misconstruing the contents of Christian civil theology. Pressures

1. See John Bowker, *The Sense of God: Sociological, Anthropological, and Psychological Approaches to the Origin of the Sense of God* (Oxford: Clarendon, 1973), and *The Religious Imagination and the Sense of God* (Oxford: Clarendon, 1978).

2. Robert John Ackerman, *Religion as Critique* (Amherst: University of Massachusetts Press, 1985), 24.

3. Kathryn Tanner, *The Politics of God: Christian Theologies and Social Justice* (Minneapolis: Fortress, 1992).

4. In this context, see the ontological reflections in Eberhard Jüngel, "The Emergence of the New," in *Theological Essays II*, ed. J. B. Webster (Edinburgh: T&T Clark, 1995), 35–58.

5. Colin E. Gunton, *A Brief Theology of Revelation* (Edinburgh: T&T Clark, 1995), 39.

exercised by prestigious general theory may be sufficiently strong that the specific substance of Christian claims about revelation and the roles played by such claims are bent out of shape in order to effect conformity with some generic idea of religious revelation. If this is so, then a good deal hangs on articulating a Christian theology of revelation with the right kind of precision; to that task we now turn.

———◈◈◈———

At the risk of blundering into some pretty hefty generalizations, we could argue that in modernity the doctrine of revelation has undergone a process of displacement. Its location in an orderly account of the Christian faith has been shifted, and in its new location it has been called upon to perform some new and rather different tasks. Little progress can be made with the notion, I suggest, until the deformity which this shift introduces is identified and treated.

The broadest outline of a diagnosis would be something like this: For a good deal of the history of Christian theology before the modern era, the concept of revelation (whether explicitly articulated or, more often, merely implied in usage and patterns of argument) has its place as part of a larger framework of convictions about God and God's relation to human persons. Although the concept is often associated with ideas of "veil-lifting," it is primarily concerned not with the communication of esoteric information but with the disclosure by God of God's character, purposes for, and requirements of humanity. So construed, the notion of revelation thus implies that knowledge of the being and ways of God is God's own gift, not the fruit of human creativity or searching. Because it is revealed, knowledge of God is the gift of divine grace and a participation in God's self-knowledge. Further, in characterizing God as the giver of knowledge of God, the concept of revelation thereby also characterizes human persons as recipients (rather than producers) of such knowledge. Accordingly, revelation and faith are closely correlated: faith is the anthropological counterpart of revelation. "Faith" is here understood not as mental assent but as a trustful, receptive disposition of the self toward the self-disclosure of an agent beyond the self. The loci of such self-disclosure are variously identified as, for example, inner illumination, Holy Scripture heard as God's Word, or the authoritative tradition of church teaching. All such loci are, however, conceived as relative to God's supreme self-disclosure in and as Jesus Christ, and to the activity of God the Holy Spirit in enabling perception of and response to God's gracious gift of knowledge of God. Understood in this way, the concept of revelation, classically conceived, is more than an epistemological category, furnishing a foundation for subsequent Christian belief. Revelation does not just answer the question of how claims to knowledge of God can be authorized; rather, it is a consequence of prior convictions about the prevenience of God in all God's relations with humanity.

With the rise of fundamental theology and philosophical prolegomena to theology in the early modern period, this coinherence of the concept of revelation with grace, Spirit, and faith began to disintegrate. The Enlightenment critique of revelation was prepared in some measure by Christian theology itself, when natural philosophy was granted the task of establishing on nontheological grounds the possibility and necessity of revelation. The effect of this development was to loosen the bonds which tie the concept of revelation to its home in the dogmatic structure of Christian theology or even to sever the bonds altogether. This happened as the notion of revelation was redeployed, being assigned a job in apologetics or foundations. This "shift from assumption to argument" is also associated in some measure with the rise of scholastic styles of theological systematization in both Protestant and Roman Catholic circles.[6] More particularly, increasing reliance on Aristotelian methods of argumentation and the quasi-Cartesian search for indubitable certainty in theology did much to undermine the correlation of revelation and faith. In effect, revelation shifts from being an implication of Christian conviction to furnishing the grounds from which Christian conviction can be deduced.

What would be involved in once again transplanting the doctrine of revelation, this time back into its native soil? To lead our thoughts, we may ponder a proposition from a contemporary theologian who more than many has endeavored to extract the doctrine of revelation from the clutter of its more recent history and to think it through

6. Ronald F. Thiemann, *Revelation and Theology: The Gospel as Narrated Promise* (Notre Dame, IN: University of Notre Dame Press, 1985), 11.

afresh: the Lutheran theologian Eberhard Jüngel. He writes: "Revelation means . . . that God is unconditioned subject of himself and as such only accessible because and insofar as he has made himself accessible."[7] What kind of descriptive expansion of that proposition might be offered?

First, the doctrine of revelation is not really a distinct doctrine at all but a function or entailment of the Christian doctrine of God. It is in that doctrine—and, more specifically, in the Christian doctrine of the Trinity—that talk of revelation has its home. In effect, we can say that "revelation" is a way of talking about the being of God, present and active among us. To speak of divine revelation is to say that God directs himself toward us and that as he does so—as his ways reach out to his creatures—he establishes knowledge of himself. In short, "revelation . . . is nothing less than God Himself."[8] Revelation is not to be understood as some separate action which God undertakes toward us, alongside God's other works of creation, preservation, or redemption, as if those other works were in and of themselves silent or simply opaque. Revelation is nothing other than the history of God's covenant with humanity in its own intrinsic perspicuity. God's actions are such that they draw us into the knowledge of God. Thus revelation is only by consequence a matter of epistemology; only secondarily does it answer the question "*How* do we know God?" It is primarily and originally a way of indicating that, in the history of Triune love, God sets himself before us so that we are drawn into fellowship with his life, a fellowship which includes knowledge. Revelation is the eloquence of divine action.

Second, as the eloquence of the action of *this* God, the God and Father of our Lord Jesus Christ, revelation is gratuitous. In it, God is indissoluble subject, undetermined and sovereignly free. *Negatively*, this is meant as a denial of some human capacity for revelation other than that which God bestows in the act of self-manifestation. There is no "natural" readiness for God's revelation independent of the event

7. Eberhard Jüngel, *Gott als Geheimnis der Welt: Zur Begründung der Theologie des Gekreuzigten im Streit zwischen Theismus und Atheismus* (Tübingen: Mohr Siebeck, 1977), 212.

8. Karl Barth, "Revelation," in *God in Action: Theological Addresses* (Edinburgh: T&T Clark, 1936), 3–19, at 12.

in which God freely and savingly makes himself present to us and
our knowledge. If God is here "subject of himself," as Jüngel puts
it, then he himself establishes all the conditions under which he may
be known. Revelation is not a dialogue between equal partners but
the majestic action of God's freedom in which he himself establishes
us as knowers. "Revelation in the Christian sense is the revelation of
a reality outside man. It is the realization of a possibility which lies
wholly in the place where the revelation takes place, not in the human
realm. It is therefore a revelation which man is powerless to bring
about of his own will."[9] *Positively,* this means that revelation is the
manifestation of the mystery or hiddenness of God. Here we need to
exercise some considerable care in expounding the doctrine of God.
To speak about the mystery or hiddenness of God is by no means to
qualify or subtract from the full force of the idea of revelation, by
asserting that there is something anterior to God as God is manifest
to us. Such shadow deities have certainly lurked in the minds—and
more particularly of the consciences—of some. But to say that God
is hidden even in revelation is to say that what is manifest is precisely
the mystery of God's being. Revelation is "a mystery, i.e., a reality
the possibility of which resides absolutely within itself."[10] Jüngel,
again, notes that this hiddenness is not to be construed as darkness
or unavailability, but as the mystery of God's splendor. "God himself
is hidden in the *light* of his own being."[11] Even in the self-revelation
of God in Jesus Christ, he writes, "the *hiddenness* of God . . . is not
thereby replaced with *absolute disclosure*."[12] Rather, "in God's revelation there occurs the (identifiable) concealment of his hiddenness."[13]
The point here is to stress that the self-revelation of God does not
mean the conversion of God into an available object of cognition;
revelation cannot be "capitalized."[14] Knowledge of God is knowledge

9. Karl Barth, "The Christian Understanding of Revelation," in *Against the
Stream: Shorter Post-War Writings, 1946–1952* (London: SCM, 1954), 203–40, at 207.
10. Barth, "Christian Understanding," 12.
11. Eberhard Jüngel, "The Revelation of the Hiddenness of God: A Contribution
to the Protestant Understanding of the Hiddenness of Divine Action," in Webster,
Theological Essays II, 120–44, at 127.
12. Jüngel, "Revelation," 129.
13. Jüngel, "Revelation," 129.
14. Barth, "Christian Understanding," 207.

of God in God's incomprehensibility, that is, in the freedom in which God lovingly bestows himself to be known as the one he is.

Third, the eloquence of divine action is directed toward us. God makes himself accessible. And "the fact that God makes himself accessible to us presupposes that God has something to do with us."[15] Revelation is fellowship freely established by God. This fellowship is the fellowship of the divine covenant: the fellowship, that is, of creator and creature, of Lord and subject, of judge and sinner, of savior and saved. It is not the mutual agreement of two equal parties but a determination made by one of the parties which unconditionally and unreservedly defines the other. The Christian understanding of revelation cannot be cast in an anthropological idiom. Though the goal of revelation is humanity, humanity is not its basis. Nor is it a fellowship in which the response of the subordinate party is either self-generated or self-referring. To respond to the gratuity with which God in revelation makes himself accessible to us is to confess, to acknowledge, to repent, to praise—all modes of the ecstasy of faith. And revelation, therefore, comes to do battle with us: to overcome our refusal to confess the sheer overwhelming goodness, beauty, and truth of God. Revelation is the overthrow of the blindness, silence, and deafness in which we refuse to be addressed and disturbed by God. That revelation does indeed overthrow us is not the least sign of that fact that it is the mercy of God.

Such, in barest outline, is revelation as a way of talking of the fellowship which God freely establishes. Two things should by now be clear. First, revelation is an ingredient within what is said about God in other loci—the doctrines of God, Christ, Spirit, and humanity, which together constitute the fabric of Christian teaching. Second, therefore, revelation is not to be made thematic on its own (especially not as a prolegomenal affair). It is an accompaniment to dogmatics proper, a way of tracing the orientation of the sovereign word and work of God to our apprehension of it in the knowledge of faith.

<hr>

15. Jüngel, *Gott als Geheimnis*, 212. [The German speaks of "humanity" rather than "us": "Daß Gott sich dem Menschen zugänglich macht, setz voraus, daß Gott den Menschen angeht."]

What is the connection between revelation, defined as the majestic, communicative presence of the Lord of the covenant, and self-critical activity on the part of the Christian community? We need to approach that question somewhat tangentially by offering a couple of critical reflections on the notion of criticism.

Our thinking about what constitutes a properly critical attitude to matters of communal belief and practice is sometimes entangled with the mythology of total critique. In recommending a responsibly "critical attitude," that is, we may be envisaging an ideal process in which we attempt entirely to transcend all viewpoints, telling ourselves that if reliable knowledge of (not simply traditional common sense about) matters is to be attained, "we must get out of ourselves, and view the world from nowhere within it."[16] But there's something wrong here.

Partly what's wrong is—as has frequently been pointed out in post-critical philosophy—the conviction that the criticism of "tradition" of necessity involves suspension of participation in its life-processes in order to attain freedom from the taint of place, time, and cultural locale. But "we shall have to acknowledge what the thinkers of the Enlightenment would have found appallingly unpalatable; namely, that examination of tradition can take place only in the context of unexamined tradition, and that in our examination, our convictions as to the facts are schooled by our traditions."[17] The reintegration of "knowing" and "social believing"[18] calls into question the ideal of total transcendence of self and tradition, the necessity of occupying "no space" as the condition for critique. Furthermore, the mythology is not unrelated to a certain anthropology, one in which criticism can turn into a kind of acquisitiveness, in which traditions are objects of resentment, above all one which can entail an ideal of "the leading intellectual cast as a heroic practitioner come down from the mountain," transcendent and sublime.[19] To put things as sharply as possible: Christian theology will

16. Thomas Nagel, *The View from Nowhere* (Oxford: Oxford University Press, 1986), 67.

17. Nicholas Wolterstorff, *John Locke and the Ethics of Belief* (Cambridge: Cambridge University Press, 1996), 246.

18. H. Richard Niebuhr, *Faith on Earth* (New Haven: Yale University Press, 1989), 36.

19. Paul A. Bové, *Intellectuals in Power: A Genealogy of Critical Humanism* (New York: Columbia University Press, 1986), 33.

have good reason to say that the mythology and its anthropology are corrupt, and at least in thinking about its own critical practice, it will seek to disentangle itself from them both. Extricating itself will involve affirming that critical practice requires the existence of a community if it is to be more than undirected skepticism. Critical theology will say of itself that "[a] theology which undertakes the limited work of understanding and criticizing within Christian history the thought and action of the church is also a theology which is dependent on the church for the constant test of its critical work."[20] This is a matter not of controlling or suppressing criticism but of *focusing* it. Criticism is never pure or transcendental; it is an aspect of contingent social and cultural systems and their patterns of self-awareness. What constitutes criticism will therefore differ widely across different social and cultural spaces. "Criticism comes in many varieties."[21] What is vital, therefore, is that criticism be pertinent. Pertinent criticism will be criticism which takes the measure of a distinctive form of human life and culture by setting it in the light of appropriate standards. In the case of Christian culture, the standards are those which emerge from the gospel. In sum: the end of critical theological inquiry is to press the question of the fidelity of all forms of Christian apostolic life, thought, and speech to the revelation of God which projects them into being. Our detour complete, we now turn to a more detailed account of the connection of revelation and criticism.

Once again, everything depends upon attaining the right kind of definition of revelation, and upon avoiding arbitrariness or generality. Revelation in the Christian sense, we have seen, is the overwhelming splendor of the being and activity of God set before us in creation and redemption. Such splendor is manifest but not possessed; like the manna in the wilderness, it is an event and not a bit of spiritual stock. Christian culture has this splendor at its center, and this splendor both *authorizes* and *disturbs*.

Revelation *authorizes*. Because of the self-communicative presence and activity of God—because in Jesus Christ the Lord of all

---

20. H. Richard Niebuhr, *The Meaning of Revelation* (New York: Macmillan, 1962), 21.

21. Charles M. Wood, *Vision and Discernment: An Orientation in Theological Study* (Atlanta: Scholars Press, 1985), 25.

things is among us through the Holy Spirit—then the church is given
authority to live, speak, and act. The church's speech and action
are eschatological, bearing witness to a different, new order of reality from far beyond the horizon of human history. The permission
and command that they be so is to be found in that fact that God's
self-manifestation has intruded upon the world. God's glory is now
visible; God's mystery, once hidden, is now manifest. And therefore
the church is commissioned to speak and act. This authorization of
the church by revelation is, crucially, something incommunicable. The
authority of revelation is not some quality which can be transmit-
ted to or deposited within the church. Revelation is, and remains, a
summons which cannot be converted into the basis of authoritarian-
ism. "To say that the God who reveals himself is a hidden God is to
confess that revelation can never constitute a body of truths which
an institution may boast of or take pride in possessing."[22]

Hence revelation *disturbs*. It is "an interruption which addresses
us."[23] As it accosts us, revelation establishes a distance—between
ourselves and our past, present, and future; between ourselves and our
traditions; between ourselves and all aspects of our settled identities.
Revelation cleaves us apart; as God's eschatological word and work,
as the presence of the divine glory, it loosens and sometimes severs
the conventions which constitute our individual and corporate selves.
To be addressed by revelation means that we may not rely unthink-
ingly on those conventions, believing them to be *simply* what is the
case. However much they form the basic and necessary structures
of our historical existence, there is no achieved symmetry between
them and the eschatological order of God. "Revelation means that
God comes to the world," and "God's coming-to-the-world means
an elemental interruption of our being-in-the-world"—including our
Christian being-in-the-world.[24] Revelation is, in short, the crisis of
Christian life and thought.

22. Paul Ricoeur, "Toward a Hermeneutic of the Idea of Revelation," in *Essays
on Biblical Interpretation*, ed. Lewis S. Mudge (Philadelphia: Fortress, 1980), 73–118,
at 95.
23. Jüngel, *Gott als Geheimnis*, 221.
24. Eberhard Jüngel, "The Dogmatic Significance of the Question of the Historical
Jesus," in Webster, *Theological Essays II*, 82–119, at 97.

What are the consequences of these kinds of affirmations for the activity of theological criticism?

Theology is not the only, or even the primary, critical undertaking of the Christian community. The church is exposed to critique above all by its hearing of the Word of God in Holy Scripture and by its celebration of Baptism and the Lord's Supper. Scripture and sacraments are critical events in the life of the church because they are points at which the Christian community is exposed to the gospel and thereby has all its speech and action set in the light of the uncontrollably alive presence of God. Whatever else the church may do by way of self-criticism—in its engagement with the voices of its non-Christian neighbors, as well as in its theology—can be only an echo of the setting forth of the gospel in word and ordinance. In theological self-criticism, the church does not invent or submit to some new standard, higher than the word which is the basis of its common life. Theological criticism is simply the church repeating to itself a judgment which has already been issued by the gospel and which, as divine judgment, is infinitely more searching, radical, and truthful than anything the church could ever generate out of its own resources or by listening to words of criticism directed to it from without.

How does theology repeat the critical presence of the gospel? The ultimate point of reference in such criticism is not abstract, not a norm derived from an external realm. Its reference point is the gospel, that is, the manifestation to the church of the majesty of God in its saving effectiveness. Theology criticizes the church (beginning, of course, with itself) by indicating the confrontation between the revelation of the gospel and its application by the church. Theological criticism is thus in one sense "immanent." It is not directed to the task of calling into question *whether*, after all, there is or should be gospel and church, or *whether* there is, after all, a Word of God to hear and obey. It is instead directed to asking about the adequacy or fidelity of the church's reception and formulation of the gospel in cult, creed, and ethos. However, this "immanent" criticism is more than simply the church as it were confronting itself with an idealized version of itself, as if the task of theology were to set a horizon before the church as a goal for striving as well as an instrument for appraisal. This sort of (hermeneutical) account of criticism has sometimes been

advocated as an alternative to the pretense to totality which, as we
have seen, afflicts much critical thought. Francis Fiorenza, for example, argues for a theology which is critical "in that it has the task
of bringing to the fore the identity of the tradition as it exists in the
paradigmatic ideals . . . of the tradition. These paradigms provide
criteria for evaluating certain developments as legitimate and others
as deformations."[25] Certainly this is greatly preferable to the abstract,
nontraditional critiques which forget that "the critic must . . . work
from within."[26] But a theology whose ultimate point of reference is
the eschatological gospel will understand itself to be responsible to
something which has a much greater measure of externality than can
be furnished by "paradigmatic ideals." Such ideals cannot completely
fulfill the need for real critical purchase on present practice, because
paradigmatic ideals are normally only available to any particular
stage of the tradition in versions of them which are amenable to
present practice. Ideals tend to offer patronage rather than furnish
the occasion for subversion. What is needed is a norm which is free,
personal, and present, and utterly resistant to incorporation. As the
eloquence of divine action, revelation furnishes this norm, and Christian theology is therefore critical because of—not despite—the fact
that it is a theology of revelation.

This is not to suggest that the norm which the gospel offers is
immediately available to us, as if all theologians had to do was to
superimpose present practice onto revelation as a template and see
where the two might differ. There are no infallible methods of theological criticism, though there are some pretty well-tested ones which
we ignore at our peril, such as exegetical or creedal fidelity. What is
crucial is that criticism be seen as a spiritual transaction which cannot be codified or made into a routine. Christian theological criticism requires of its practitioners the same skills as any other kind of
theology, because it *is* simply Christian theology about the business
of appraisal rather than description. It requires the same attentiveness, the same self-distrust, the same readiness for fresh conversion,

25. Francis Schüssler Fiorenza, *Foundational Theology: Jesus and the Church*
(New York: Crossroad, 1984), 305–6.
26. R. G. Collingwood, *An Essay on Philosophical Method* (Oxford: Clarendon,
1933), 219.

above all, the same prayer for the coming of the Holy Spirit to disable the dullness of our blinded sight. Critical theology is thus a mode of reflective attention to the gospel, one which directs that attention to the possible fissures between the gospel and our inhabitation of it. Therein, it simply reiterates God's repudiation of our idolatries.

⟾◈⟾

To sum things up, we may listen to the closing words of a great and nowadays unjustly neglected book, T. F. Torrance's magisterial study *Theological Science*. One of the excellences of that book is that in it Torrance grasps that Christian dogmatics is critical precisely because and in the measure with which it is itself: Christian dogmatics. Dogmatics is not a rampart against taking seriously the possibility one might be wrong but one of the things that happens to our minds when revelation breaks through our defenses and makes us repent. Torrance writes thus:

> It must not be forgotten that the sole Object of dogmatic statements is the Datum of divine Revelation which does not cease to be God's own Being and Act in His Self-giving, and therefore is not something that passes over into the inner spiritual states of the Church's experience or into its historical consciousness and subjectivity. . . . All this forces dogmatics to be a highly critical science in which all theological statements are to be severely tested to determine whether, in their correlation with the subject and in their claim to speak of God, Father, Son and Holy Spirit, they really do intend God, whether it really is Christ that they mean, and whether they really do distinguish the Holy Spirit from the human spirit. Dogmatics, like the Church itself, stands or falls with sheer respect for the Majesty and Freedom of God in His Word and for the transcendence of His Truth over all our statements about it even when we do our utmost to make them aright . . . in accordance with the rectitude of the Truth itself as it comes to light in our inquiry into the divine Revelation.[27]

If that is true, then theological criticism requires humility as a basic virtue. And it is to the virtues of the theologian that we will turn in the final lecture.

27. Thomas F. Torrance, *Theological Science* (Oxford: Oxford University Press, 1969), 351–52.

6

Habits

Cultivating the Theologian's Soul

So far in these lectures, we've been examining the politics of theology and the critical theory of theology. We've looked, that is, at the institutional forms within which theology of the kind which I am recommending can struggle to find some sort of home (however temporary), as well as the sorts of practices of critical self-evaluation which provide one of the ways in which theology is pulled up short in its almost inevitable straying into ideology.

In this final lecture, I want to bring matters a bit nearer home and offer an idealized portrait of the theologian—a picture of the sort of persons that theologians (that is, we) might aim to become. The task is what we might call an *ethics* of theology or, perhaps better, an *anthropology* of the theologian: a sketch of the human striving and suffering which are involved in doing theology well. I want to pick up the suggestion which I made at the very beginning of the series of lectures that the flourishing of the theological culture of Christian faith requires, among other things, the cultivation of persons: good theology demands good theologians. Thinking and speaking well of the God of the Christian gospel involves the rather bruising business

of acquiring and practicing certain habits of mind, heart, and will—
"bruising," because those habits shape the soul as it were against the
grain. They lead us in a way we would rather not go; they press us to
become what we would rather not be. "It is necessary," says Augustine in *De doctrina Christiana*, "that we should be led by the *fear of
God* to seek the knowledge of His will. . . . It is necessary to have our
hearts subdued by *piety*."[1] Our theme today is the impact made on
the existence of the theologian by that necessity—so all-consuming
in its demands, so rewarding in ways that we can scarcely imagine.

There probably should be a question mark after my subtitle. For
it's crucial at the beginning of exploring what's involved in the process
of cultivating theologians that, in one very important sense, it is an
impossibility. We can no more make ourselves or others into theologians than we can raise the dead; indeed, it's precisely because we
cannot raise ourselves from the dead that we cannot make ourselves
or others into theologians. The first and last act of theological existence is crying to God: "Be pleased, O God, to deliver me!" (Ps. 70:1).
In the intervening space between that first and last act of theological
existence, the cultivation of the theologian has its place; but it will
only do its task well if it keeps a firm eye on the fact that all the cultivation in the world can never be anything other than an appeal to
God for the miracle of mercy. Recommending the primacy of prayer
for the Christian preacher near the end of *De doctrina Christiana*,
Augustine says this: "He who is anxious both to know and to teach
should learn all that is to be taught, and acquire such a faculty for
speech as is suitable for a divine. But when the hour for speech arrives, let him reflect upon that saying of our Lord's. . . . 'Take no
thought how or what ye shall speak; for it shall be given you in that
same hour what ye shall speak. For it is not ye that speak, but the
Spirit of your Father which speaketh in you.'"[2] Augustine, of course,
is no despiser of human skills: one of the refrains of *De doctrina* is
the folly of those who despise human instruction and refuse to let
themselves be shaped in the school of human abilities. Nevertheless,
Augustine knows that in the end both we and our speech are in the
hands of God and that to make talk of God into a human project

1. Augustine, *On Christian Doctrine* (Edinburgh: T&T Clark, 1873), II.7.9.
2. Augustine, *On Christian Doctrine*, IV.15.32.

without reference to the utterance of the Spirit is to misunderstand the point of the gospel.

Good theology demands good theologians. To talk in these terms is—emphatically—not a matter of "existentializing" theology, so that the only thing that really matters in theological work is the inner affective states of the theological practitioner. Certainly dispositions do matter, and inattention to them is damaging. But of itself inner authenticity secures nothing; moreover, it is not authenticity to self but authenticity to Christ and the gospel which is to define Christian theological existence. So my claim is not merely that theologians ought to cultivate certain modulations of their inner lives (though I think they should), but more that Christian theological existence is nothing other than a form of Christian existence, standing under exactly the same total claim of the gospel. Part of what is required as a response to that claim is readiness for the kinds of personal growth and change which inevitably afflict us in engagement with God. Engagement with God means being sufficiently grasped, disturbed, or troubled by the gospel and its dispute with us, that we are provoked (however unwillingly) to learn how to think and live differently. But part of the difference that we are to learn is the dawning of the realization that "learning how to think and live differently" is not just a matter of adding on new attitudes or adopting new patterns of action; it involves abandoning my mastery of myself and receiving myself anew from God. Good theologians are those whose life and thought are caught up in the process of being slain and made alive by the gospel and of acquiring and exercising habits of mind and heart which take very seriously the gospel's provocation.

<hr />

I have already tried to describe some aspects of the current practice of theology and the institutions in which that practice occurs which may make us reluctant to press very hard the sort of claims which I have just been advancing. There can be very few who are involved in theological work who are not in some measure preoccupied with questions of the relation of academic theology to the nurture of piety. Nevertheless, mainstream academic institutions (sometimes ecclesiastically sponsored) have not always found it easy to affirm that theological activity requires the cultivation not only of technical skills but also of habits of the soul. The reasons for our reluctance are normally invisible, but once unearthed, they often present a combination of philosophical and educational instincts.

The philosophical instinct leads us to assert that the rationality which scholarship requires is independent of character and conviction. If that is so, then learning the truth does not involve a shaping of the self or any kind of readiness for formation. What it requires is, rather, the unhindered exercise of innate capacities for the exercise of reason, on the principle that truth "can be discovered or confirmed by any adequately intelligent person."[3] Reasonableness is thus isolatable from the context of the life-project of an individual or group. Thereby it is at one and the same time restricted and elevated: restricted in that its exercise is identified only with a narrow band of intellectual activities (representation and judgment); elevated, in that that band of activities comes to be intellectually and, indeed, humanly basic, much more so than any contingent characteristics of persons or forms of common life. Throughout these lectures, I have been quarreling with this account of rationality. In part, this is because I believe reason is best understood as a historical, not a natural, concept. Reason is reason in context, standing in relation to social customs and traditions with their modes of inquiry and evaluation. Beyond this, I have also sought to identify how this "naturalized" account of rationality is in fact underwritten by a set of ideals about the nature of human personhood. In these ideals, reasonableness is the expression in the cognitive realm of a certain account of liberty as undetermined by situation, an account whose inspiration is as much moral and political as it is epistemological. Charles Taylor describes this anthropology as a "picture of the subject as ideally disengaged, that is, as free and rational to the extent that he has fully distinguished himself from the natural and social worlds, so that his identity is no longer to be defined in terms of what lies outside him in these worlds."[4] The cumulative suggestion of a good deal of recent philosophy has been that

3. Alasdair MacIntyre, *Three Rival Versions of Moral Enquiry: Encyclopedia, Genealogy, and Tradition* (Notre Dame, IN: University of Notre Dame Press, 1990), 60.
4. Charles Taylor, "Overcoming Epistemology," in *Philosophical Arguments* (Cambridge: Harvard University Press, 1995), 1–19, at 7.

this epistemology and its anthropology have failed, and therefore that the cultivation of reason will of necessity also involve the cultivation of certain habits of mind through participation in and drawing on the stores of knowledge which belong to a shared life-world.

This is connected with the second, educational instinct which may make it difficult for us to think of the life of the mind as inseparable from the shaping of the soul.[5] If reasonableness is restricted to "adequate intelligence," then educating reason is not the formation of the self but is teaching reason how to extricate itself from all that is merely contingent and customary. The required ascesis is that of reason's separation from body, society, and history so that it can represent the world to itself in thought and language. Thus one influential understanding of education works with an ideal of "indifference," in two senses. First, the teacher may not impose a way of life and the student may not expect to be encouraged to adopt any particular vision of the world. And second, therefore, education has done its job when the student has learned the skills of critical appraisal of the particular, of "difference," by reference to reason's universal norms. But again: if reason is historical, then its exercise of necessity involves the inhabitation of a tradition, a space in the historical world; and if that is true, then the education of reason involves learning the skills, habits, and roles which are appropriate to living in that world, intending and achieving its ends.

The objections to the importance of formation which are still ingrained in some educational practice have been seriously (and effectively) undermined in the neo-Aristotelian philosophy of virtue which has been so influential on some dominant styles of moral and political philosophy. Not surprisingly, a number of recent accounts of the nature of Christian theology and theological education have found these wider developments to be companionable, suggesting that the acquisition and use of Christian language and concepts involves moral, emotional, and spiritual growth. It is, moreover, scarcely

5. For important work in this connection, see Martha C. Nussbaum, *Cultivating Humanity: A Classical Defense of Reform in Liberal Education* (Cambridge: Harvard University Press, 1997); Amélie Oksenberg Rorty, "Moral Imperialism vs. Moral Conflict: Conflicting Aims of Education," in *Can Virtue Be Taught?*, ed. Barbara Darling-Smith (Notre Dame, IN: University of Notre Dame Press, 1993), 33–51.

possible to envisage such growth apart from some kind of participation in the corporate activities of the Christian community (such as worship) in which Christian roles and meanings are acted out with the measure of density which we require if we are to learn how to make use of them with any degree of accuracy or creativity. If that is so, the argument goes, a theological school involves much more than instruction in the use of certain tools (languages, modes of historical inquiry, skills of conceptual analysis, and so on). A theological school is a school for the formation of gospel character, a community of learners engaged in common enterprises which build up patterns of fellowship through which they become people with certain habits of life and mind—certain structured and not immediately reflective ways of reading the world and acting within it. Habits form virtues, and virtues are the content of character. To be a theological learner is to be one engaged in the business of inculcating the habits, learning the virtues, and so coming to have one's life engraved (usually painfully) with a certain "character."

So far, I hope, so good—however much what actually goes on in theological institutions may lag pretty far behind. But is it a model we want to embrace wholeheartedly? It is undoubtedly infinitely superior to an account of theology and theological learning which is wedded to "the anorexic form of the critical principle" which has come to dominate a lot of higher learning.[6] But we need to beware a certain naivete. The first reason for this is political. Schools of character are places of power, often exercised in petty and damaging ways. What counts as a fitting habit or virtue, what stands as the norm for character development, is not immediately transparent to us but nearly always set before us through the interpreting and authorizing acts of others who claim greater or lesser degrees of sanction for the versions of reality which they seek to promote. None of this is avoidable; nor are the inevitable contests which it produces in principle insoluble, however demanding on our resources. But we do well to remember that idealizing the processes of character formation may be a means of immunizing it against questioning, including the questioning summons of the gospel.

6. Edward Farley, *The Fragility of Knowledge: Theological Education in the Church and the University* (Philadelphia: Fortress, 1988), 15.

A second reason for thinking hard about the ideas of habit, character formation, and virtue, which will detain us for most of the rest of this lecture, is theological. In the opening lecture we noted that the ideas of "culture" and "practice" could not be adopted wholesale in talking of the nature of Christian theology, because the "region" in which Christian theology operates is that amazing eschatological space constituted by the presence and action of God in Christ through the Spirit: Christian faith is as much an anti-culture as a culture. Again, in looking at the notion of "tradition," I tried to suggest that the Christian tradition is not a steady state but a mobile set of responses to the apostolic imperative. So also here: we need to ensure that any account of the character of the theologian is not tied to an anthropology of immanence, in which the sheer freedom and otherness of the gospel is compromised.

The most acute questions here are therefore: In what sense are the virtues of the theologian to be attributed to him- or herself? To what extent are the habits of mind and soul which inform good theological practice internal to the theological practitioner? Asked the other way around: In what ways does the goodness or excellence of the theologian remain external to him or her—as a movement of divine grace which touches the theologian's person and activity but which does not in any straightforward way we can describe become part of his or her human make-up?[7]

These are questions about moral psychology of the utmost complexity, about which different traditions in Christianity have thought in widely divergent ways. The kinds of answers that one gives will depend on a couple of factors. They will depend, first, on the overall shape of the doctrinal configuration within which a Christian moral psychology is located. Are the leading doctrinal motifs, for instance, those of anthropology (particularly those of an anthropology of inwardness or self-realization, as they often have been in modern theology)? Or is the psychology set within a different doctrinal order: one in which creation or providence plays a leading role, or one in which redemption in Christ is considered definitive of what it means

7. For a quite different account from mine, see Huston Smith, "Educating the Intellect: On Opening the Eye of the Heart," in Darling-Smith, *Can Virtue Be Taught?*, 17–31.

to be and act humanly? These different configurations will have different evaluations of how "internal" the virtues of the theologian are and* will develop different strategies for preventing what may be considered the "immanentizing" dangers of any account of virtue. Thus the moral space within which the Christian theologian's existence and activity take place will be differently constructed according to the different tracts of Christian teaching to which appeal is made in its interpretation. Second, the sort of answer one gives to the question of the internality or otherwise of Christian virtues will also depend on one's account of the virtues themselves. It will depend on what virtues are thought most important for theologians to develop and on the particular content that is ascribed to such virtues: by what particular habits are they constituted? It will, further, depend on the way in which different virtues are ordered, some being accorded ascendancy over others. To put things at their simplest: because a Christian moral psychology ultimately rests on an account of what Christianity is, so also does a portrait of what the Christian theologian ought to look like.

My own account of the matter—as by now you will no doubt have guessed—takes its lead from the proposal that Christian theological existence falls under the same rule as the rest of Christian existence. The rule was enunciated with stunning clarity by Calvin: *non nostri sumus, sed Domini* [We are not our own, but the Lord's].[8] Any comprehensive mapping of that rule and the range of its applications would involve us in examining some lengthy tracts of Christology, soteriology, and pneumatology—teaching about the Word's

---

*[The section of text that follows from here until the point signaled at the following asterisk was inadvertently omitted from the version published in *Stimulus* 7, no. 1 (1999), 17. It has been supplied by Professor Davidson's copy of Webster's original typescript.]

8. John Calvin, *Institutes,* III.vii.1 [evoking 1 Cor. 6:19. The Latin word order in *Iohannis Calvini Opera Selecta*, vol. IV: *Institutionis Christianae religionis 1559, librum III continens*, ed. Wilhelm Niesel and Peter Barth (Munich: Kaiser, 1931), 151.16 is *nostri non sumus, sed Domini*; cf. John Calvin, *Institutes of the Christian Religion*, ed. John T. McNeill, trans. Ford Lewis Battles (Philadelphia: Westminster, 1960), 689–90. Webster refers his readers to his elaboration of the axiom in the present lecture in "Christ, Church, and Reconciliation," in John Webster, *Word and Church, Essays in Christian Dogmatics* (New York: T&T Clark, 2001; 2nd ed., 2016), 211–30, at 228n39.]

assumption of humanity, the saving power of that act, and the union with Christ which is effected by the giving of the Holy Spirit. Making appeal to this doctrinal material would ensure that a moral anthropology attained the right kind of Christian determinacy and did not fall into the trap of letting itself become one member (usually the inferior one) of a coalition with other, more prestigious understandings of the human person. But appeal to Christology and pneumatology would also be made in order to ensure that the incommunicability of God is maintained in our moral psychology—so that God and the human person do not shade into one another. Even in the intimacy of God's fellowship with the redeemed, the unassailable freedom and majesty of his condescension is not broken down. The existence of the Christian theologian is what it is because it is summoned forth and maintained in being by that act of condescension. All of which is simply to repeat that Christian theological existence is eschatological. The point is worth pausing over.

"If any one is in Christ, [that person] is a new creation: the old has passed away, behold, the new has come" (2 Cor. 5:17). The human lives of Christian believers are a "converted" reality. That is to say, their existence as the redeemed people of God in a redeemed creation is neither identical with nor a straightforward extension of unredeemed existence: it is something *other*. At its basis lie disruption, discontinuity, the abandonment of one mode of existence and the taking up of another—a transition graphically represented by the baptismal movement from death to life. Converted existence is existence which arises from a complete and radical interruption of the continuities of human life, an interruption which at once judges and sets aside and also liberates for a truthful existence which entirely transcends the limitations of that which it replaces.

The change, in other words, is absolute, in that converted existence is not derivable from that which it replaces: How can life be derived from death? It is not just a matter of the exchange of one mode of existence for another, more serviceable, perhaps, but not in the end radically different. Converted existence is not a relative rearrangement of aspects of human existence but the bringing about of that which is new: Paul's language of new *creation* is to be taken with full seriousness at this point. The disjunction between the old and the new entails, therefore,* the exclusion of certain ways of under-standing the continuity of the self. Certainly there is continuity at the formal level: the subject to whom converted existence is ascribed is in identifiable bodily and temporal continuity with him- or herself as a unique subject of ascription. But the self's continuity is not such that the old and the new are points on a continuum, different dispositions of a subject which is self-identical prior to or apart from or behind the history of its transformation by God. Nor is the self's continuity such that we have to say that the person has *in nuce, in potentia,* all that it will become in the course of its history, including the radi-cal alteration of that history by God. Continuity is not guaranteed, that is, by deriving the subject's end from some supposed resources with which that subject is endowed by virtue of its creatureliness. Rather, continuity is discerned from the opposite direction—from the divinely accomplished eschatological transformation of the subject, in the light of which an orderly narrative of the subject's identity is possible.

Because the convertedness of human life is underivable from all that has gone before, our account of it has to talk of divine agency as its cause. We are here faced with a reality of irreducible newness, and so language of God's creativity is indispensable. For Christian theology, language about divine creativity is not only language about the original ordering of creation by divine agency but also (indeed, primarily) language about God's decisive reordering of creation in Jesus Christ, supremely in his resurrection from the dead. Thus Paul can define God as the one "who gives life to the dead and calls into existence the things that do not exist" (Rom. 4:17), linking the cre-ativity of God to the fact that God is the one "who raised Christ Jesus from the dead" (8:11). The resurrection of Jesus constitutes the new creation, and it is by participation in his resurrection through the life-bestowing activity of the Spirit that women and men attain to that "newness of life," the eschatological existence in which their true being is found.

"Eschatological existence" is thus not the realization of latent human possibilities but a *gift,* realized by an external agency which

*[The text hereafter continues as published.]

destroys and makes alive. The *potentia aliena* by which this is brought
about is the existence of the human person Jesus. At this point, the
logic of Christian confession commits us, in my judgment, to affirming that that human existence, that particular, nameable human
identity is, in all its particularity, not a mere contingent fragment of
world-occurrence but in some sense shares in the absoluteness of
God. The life, death, and resurrection of Jesus constitute *the* context
in which all other human living and dying are to be set; his history is a
judgment which renders relative all other frames of reference. It resists
being "placed" within existing schemes, for it functions as a locus of
judgment upon any attempt at comprehension. This, it seems to me,
is what the New Testament's link between Jesus's resurrection and
his Lordship presses us toward: as the risen Lord, he renders relative,
and is not himself relativized, since God "raised him from the dead
and made him sit at his right hand in the heavenly places, far above
all rule and authority and power and dominion, and above every
name that is named, not only in this age but also in that which is to
come; and he has put all things under his feet" (Eph. 1:20–22; cf. Col.
1:16–20). As the risen one, sharing in the limitlessness of God, Jesus is
"that than which nothing greater can be conceived." Accordingly, the
eschatological, "regenerate" reality of human life has priority in our
determination of what human life is like, a priority in view of which
the "unregenerate" state can only be seen as essentially negative, as
a privation. For if it is true that Jesus's history as the risen one is
"the pre-history and post-history of all our individual lives,"[9] if it is
true that to be human is to subsist in the reality of Jesus Christ, then
human beings are most fundamentally defined not by what they have
been, nor by what they are, nor by what they make of themselves, but
by what, under the impulse of the gospel, they *become*.

How do such christological-eschatological affirmations shape
Christian moral psychology? A whole string of New Testament assertions press for our attention at this point: "So you also must consider yourselves dead to sin and alive to God in Jesus Christ" (Rom.
6:11); "He is the source of your life in Christ Jesus, whom God made

---

9. Ingolf U. Dalferth, "Karl Barth's Eschatological Realism," in *Karl Barth: Centenary Essays*, ed. S. W. Sykes (Cambridge: Cambridge University Press, 1989), 14–45,
at 27.

our wisdom, our righteousness and sanctification and redemption"
(1 Cor. 1:30); "it is no longer I who live, but Christ who lives in
me" (Gal. 2:20); "and you he made alive" (Eph. 2:1); "and you, who
were dead in trespasses and the uncircumcision of your flesh, God
made alive together with him" (Col. 2:13). Such assertions are to be
taken as statements about the being of the Christian; but spelling
out their ontological force requires a decisive break with some basic
metaphysical assumptions which underlie our psychology. Above all,
what is required is a way of thinking about human existence in which
central place is held by the redemption of creation, established in
Jesus Christ and realized in the sphere of creaturely existence by his
converting presence in the Spirit. We need, that is, an ontology and
anthropology of redemption, in which creation is seen as a history,
with its teleology governed not so much by its past ordering as by
its future consummation, secured in the redeeming work of Christ.
The "eager longing" and "groaning in travail" of the creation (Rom.
8:19, 22) are, on this account, determinative of what the creation is:
that reality which God is bringing into being as he makes it new.

Eschatological existence will, therefore, be "eccentric" (what the
classical tradition called "anhypostatic"), having its center not in
itself but in another. This, once more, may lead us to make some
rather serious qualifications of the language of character, virtue, and
habit to talk of Christian and theological existence. In his *Outline of
a Theory of Practice*, Pierre Bourdieu defines a habit as "a durably
installed generative principle of regulated improvisations."[10] But can
the graces of the Spirit be "durably installed"? The theological traditions of the Reformation, and especially the anthropology of Luther,
have serious reserves about speaking in such ways, precisely because
what it is God's to give cannot be converted into dispositions or, by
some process of transfer of properties from God to humanity, made
into routines by its recipients. The point of this protest (however puz-
zling it may be to spell it out as a moral psychology) is to alert us to
the limits of the language of habit, virtue, and character. If Christian
existence is eschatological, if the center of its life and endeavors is in
the utter sufficiency of another, then—like the apostolicity or holiness

10. Pierre Bourdieu, *Outline of a Theory of Practice* (Cambridge: Cambridge
University Press, 1977), 78.

of the church—the life and acts of the believer are wholly taken up by indicating that which he supremely is and does.

> To exist theologically is to be a person under the promise and in the expectation of new life. Under this promise one is called, one is inserted into the new situation before God that is opened up by God's condemning and saving judgment. One is inserted into the hidden history of Jesus Christ in the world. That *is* the living space in which our being human is "located" and "takes place." "For you died, and your life is hidden with Christ in God" (Colossians 3:3 [NKJV]). That is a categorical indicative, the content of the judgment of God upon our existence and at the same time the communication of new life.[11]

What does all this mean for the anatomy of the theologian? Maybe we can answer that question by first of all asking a further question: In what sense can theological existence be cultivated? The first thing to say is that it can't. Theological existence is existence in the theater of grace, life under the determination of the self-giving presence of God the Holy Spirit. There is no technology of the Spirit, no moral or intellectual or even spiritual performance which will automatically make us into theologians. What there is—much to our disappointment, usually—is prayer. At the heart of theological existence is calling upon God. Prayer is not to be thought of functionally or instrumentally. It is not a means to an end; it is not some kind of contemplative clearing of the mind or spirit, a positioning of oneself more accurately before the intellectual task. Even less is prayer part of a benign ambience of religiosity which bathes our scholarly efforts with its light (a daft idea if ever I heard one). Prayer is speech addressed to God in which we ask for help with an urgency and intensity which only make sense if we really are in dire straits. Prayer is that basic human action which corresponds to our incapacity, to our unsuitability for what is required of us, and therefore to the utter necessity of the merciful intervention of God. To pray is to be human

---

11. Gerhard Sauter, *Eschatological Rationality: Theological Issues in Focus* (Grand Rapids: Baker, 1996), 197–98.

in the theater of grace. In his celebrated chapter on prayer in book 3 of the *Institutes*, Calvin writes thus:

> We clearly see how destitute and devoid of all good things man is, and how he lacks all aids to salvation. Therefore, if he seeks resources to succor him in his need, he must go outside himself and get them elsewhere. . . . The Lord willingly and freely reveals himself in his Christ. For in Christ he offers all happiness in place of our misery, all wealth in place of our neediness; in him he opens to us the heavenly treasures that our whole faith may contemplate his beloved Son, our whole expectation depends upon him, and our whole hope cleave to and rest in him. . . . But after we have been instructed by faith to recognize that whatever we need and whatever we lack is in God, and in our Lord Jesus Christ, in whom the Father willed all the fullness of his bounty to abide so that we may all draw from it as from an overflowing spring, it remains for us to seek in him, and in prayers to ask of him, what we have learned to be in him. . . . Just as faith is born from the gospel, so through it our hearts are trained to call upon God's name.[12]

Thus understood—as a primary correlate of faith, as caught up within sin's impoverishment of us and the reversal of that impoverishment by the treasure of divine grace—prayer underlines the destitution of the theologian when faced with the task of thought and speech of God.

Speaking of prayer in this way relativizes the notion of the formation of the theologian's character. But it does not mean that "formation" is to be abandoned as, at best, superfluous and, at worst, a kind of hubris in which we arrogate to ourselves what is properly the work of God alone. It simply means that formation shares what Barth calls the "vocative" structure of the Christian life in its entirety.[13] Formation is not a natural therapeutic process, a skill in managing the soul through which certain habits can be engendered. The fundamental dynamic of formation is appeal for the gracious action of God. Training in custom, acquisition of habits, the slow and unsteady growth into virtue—none of this culture of the theologian is anything other than an entry into

12. Calvin, *Institutes*, III.xx.1, at 850–51.
13. Karl Barth, *The Christian Life: Church Dogmatics IV/4—Lecture Fragments* (Edinburgh: T&T Clark, 1981), 51.

the movement whose culminating moment is appeal to God in prayer. Formation, cultivating the soul, is a waiting on God, a waiting which is itself enabled and which looks to God in humble expectancy.

If this is true, where does it leave us with regard to giving a portrait of what the theologian ought to be? One way of proceeding would be to give a characterization of the Christian life as a whole: faith, hope, delight in and amazement at God, zeal, watchfulness, praise, mortification, and much more. Any selection of virtues for the purposes of portraying theological existence is bound to be occasional—that is, an idealized picture which emphasizes certain features over others because in the present context they are considered to be of prime importance. However much what happens in theology is only a little episode in the wider history of the apostolic community, there is only really the theologian *here*. In our present situation, I would hope that of all the things for which the theologian might pray, he or she might ask for an especial measure of three things.

The first is fear of God. Little progress is possible in theology unless one's will is broken, in order to be redirected by God to the true ends of human flourishing. Saying this, of course, opens one up to all manner of calumny: of hostility to the human good, of promoting servility, of that "lack of resolution and courage" which Kant thought makes human beings into nothing better than "domestic cattle."[14] But Christian wisdom distinguishes reverence from the sheer terror of God which is dread of punishment or loathing at being discovered. Fear of God is the result of finding oneself set in the light of God's truth, and so is a readiness for that dying to self which is the dark side of resurrection. In theological work, fear of God means realizing that what we do when we do speak and think about the God of the gospel is a matter for wonder rather than curiosity. We may not take a look at the matter of Christian theology as if it could be viewed from a distance, as if we could take up an attitude toward

14. Immanuel Kant, "What Is Enlightenment?," in *On History*, ed. Lewis White Beck (New York: Macmillan, 1963), 3–10, at 3. [Webster may not have known in preparing the lectures that the University of Otago (in common with a number of other educational institutions around the world) has as its motto *Sapere aude*—"Dare to be wise" (Horace, *Epistles* 1.2.40)—famously cited at the start of Kant's essay (p. 3) as the motto of *Aufklärung*.]

it, even perhaps patronize it with our attention, or maybe simply abandon it at will. Thought and speech about God are propelled into existence by a question posed to us. And the question which is posed to us is not a simple proposition with which we may play until our interest falls upon something else more enticing; it is the question posed by the living, judging presence of God. Theological existence is existence in the light of the indicative and imperative of the first commandment.

To see a little more of how this might be fleshed out in theological practice, we turn to the second ideal characteristic: a patient teachability or deference on the part of the theologian. Deference to what? Deference to the gospel, finally, as the self-testimony of the risen Christ but also deference to the company of those who have studied, suffered, and prayed the gospel in the catholic community of faith. This is part of what is meant by orthodoxy. Rather than thinking of orthodoxy as mute subscription to dogmas, it is much better to understand it as participation in a shared, comprehensive culture, within whose scope one learns how to read the world by filling out certain roles, pondering and making use of certain ideas, figuring out how to speak a certain language well, in one or another of its different local dialects. Belonging precedes suspicion. As a principle of action, suspicion rarely serves us well, because it is not compatible with the sort of courtesy and readiness for instruction by which we learn how to move around a particular space. As the Dominican theologian Aidan Nichols puts it, "The first prerequisite of the theologian is not originality so much as docility, an active, eager, lively willingness to be formed, instructed and inspired."[15] One of the most telling expressions of this will be a deference to the canon of Christian texts, both biblical and traditional; such deference is, I believe, equally a mode of defiance, a way of giving the lie to the great illusion which still returns to haunt us, namely that (again, in Kant's words) "our age is . . . the age of criticism, and to criticism everything must submit."[16]

15. Aidan Nichols, "T. S. Eliot and Yves Congar on the Nature of Tradition," in *Scribe of the Kingdom: Essays on Theology and Culture*, vol. 1 (London: Sheed & Ward, 1994), 78–89, at 87.
16. Immanuel Kant, preface to the first edition, *Critique of Pure Reason* (Garden City, NY: Doubleday, 1966), xxiv.

If, nevertheless, that sounds rather constricting, let me add very briefly a third characteristic: freedom from self-preoccupation. Orthodoxy becomes dangerous when its maintenance is a matter of self-protection: anxious patrolling of the perimeter fence around our cultural space, sniping at intruders or at any poor souls trying to escape. But there is a mode of cheerful belonging to a tradition which is not obsessive in its attachments, but rather regards them with a free, unharassed relativity. Perhaps the best word for this is "irony"—by which we do not mean skepticism or refusal of belonging but a genuine freedom within commitment which has learned the wisdom to distinguish one's own bit of the tradition from God. This healthy irony cannot be exercised too early; if it is, it usually descends into flippancy. It is properly something grown into and entails learning a measure of detachment from any one articulation of the gospel, usually through making oneself familiar with other articulations and seeing the kinds of apostolic, holy life and thought they promote.

I suppose one should end a series of lectures with a sort of rhetorical flourish. Such flourishes are beyond my abilities, I'm afraid, but the expression of gratitude is not. I am indeed grateful for the invitation to be among you, for your patience in listening to these strange ideas, and for offering me the opportunity to think about them myself.

We have talked much of prayer in this lecture, and it will therefore not, I hope, be entirely inappropriate to end with a prayer. It is the collect for the ninth Sunday after Trinity in the Sarum missal, rendered into English for Cranmer's first prayer book in 1549, and it is a prayer which I sometimes think of as the prayer *par excellence* of the theologian: "Grant to us, Lord, we beseech thee, the spirit to think and do always such things as be rightful; that we, who cannot do anything that is good without thee, may by thee be enabled to live according to thy will; through Jesus Christ our Lord."

Bibliography

WORKS ARE LISTED as cited in the lectures. In many instances, the texts are now available in more recent versions or collections.

Ackerman, Robert John. *Religion as Critique.* Amherst: University of Massachusetts Press, 1985.

Augustine. *On Christian Doctrine.* Translated by J. F. Shaw. In *The Works of Aurelius Augustine, Bishop of Hippo: A New Translation,* vol. 9. Edited by Marcus Dods. Edinburgh: T&T Clark, 1873.

Bacon, Francis. *The Advancement of Learning.* Edited with an introduction by G. W. Kitchin. London: Dent, 1915.

Barth, Karl. *Anselm: Fides Quaerens Intellectum; Anselm's Proof of the Existence of God in the Context of His Theological Scheme.* Translated by Ian W. Robertson. London: SCM, 1960.

———. *The Christian Life: Church Dogmatics IV/4—Lecture Fragments.* Translated by Geoffrey W. Bromiley. Edinburgh: T&T Clark, 1981.

———. "The Christian's Place in Society." In *The Word of God and the Word of Man,* translated by Douglas Horton, 272–327. London: Hodder & Stoughton, 1928.

———. "The Christian Understanding of Revelation." In *Against the Stream: Shorter Post-War Writings, 1946–1952,* translated by E. M. Delacour and Stanley Godman, edited by Ronald Gregor Smith, 203–40. London: SCM, 1954.

————. *Church Dogmatics*. Vol. I/1: *The Doctrine of the Word of God*. Translated by G. W. Bromiley. Edited by G. W. Bromiley and T. F. Torrance. 2nd ed. Edinburgh: T&T Clark, 1975.

————. *Church Dogmatics*. Vol. IV/1: *The Doctrine of Reconciliation*. Translated by G. W. Bromiley. Edited by G. W. Bromiley and T. F. Torrance. Edinburgh: T&T Clark, 1956.

————. *Church Dogmatics*. Vol. IV/3: *The Doctrine of Reconciliation*. Translated by G. W. Bromiley. Edited by G. W. Bromiley and T. F. Torrance. Edinburgh: T&T Clark, 1961.

————. *Ethics*. Translated by Geoffrey W. Bromiley. Edited by Dietrich Braun. Edinburgh: T&T Clark, 1981.

————. "Revelation." In *God in Action: Theological Addresses*, translated by E. G. Homrighausen and Karl J. Ernst, with an introduction by Josias Friedl, 3–19. Edinburgh: T&T Clark, 1936.

Bourdieu, Pierre. *Outline of a Theory of Practice*. Translated by Richard Nice. Cambridge: Cambridge University Press, 1977.

Bové, Paul A. *Intellectuals in Power: A Genealogy of Critical Humanism*. New York: Columbia University Press, 1986.

Bowker, John. *The Religious Imagination and the Sense of God*. Oxford: Clarendon, 1978.

————. *The Sense of God: Sociological, Anthropological, and Psychological Approaches to the Origin of the Sense of God*. Oxford: Clarendon, 1973.

Brown, Delwin. *Boundaries of Our Habitations: Tradition and Theological Construction*. Albany, NY: SUNY Press, 1994.

Bruns, Gerald L. *Inventions: Writing, Textuality, and Understanding in Literary History*. New Haven: Yale University Press, 1982.

Calvin, John. *Institutes of the Christian Religion*. Translated by Ford Lewis Battles. Edited by John T. McNeill. Philadelphia: Westminster, 1960.

Charry, Ellen. *By the Renewing of Your Minds*. Oxford: Oxford University Press, 1997.

Collingwood, R. G. *An Essay on Philosophical Method*. Oxford: Clarendon, 1933.

Dalferth, Ingolf U. "Karl Barth's Eschatological Realism." In *Karl Barth: Centenary Essays*, edited by S. W. Sykes, 14–45. Cambridge: Cambridge University Press, 1989.

Farley, Edward. *The Fragility of Knowledge: Theological Education in the Church and the University*. Philadelphia: Fortress, 1988.

Fiorenza, Francis Schüssler. *Foundational Theology: Jesus and the Church*. New York: Crossroad, 1984.

Fowl, Stephen E., and L. Gregory Jones. *Reading in Communion: Scripture and Ethics in Christian Life*. Grand Rapids: Eerdmans, 1991.

Frei, Hans W. *The Identity of Jesus Christ: The Hermeneutical Bases of Dogmatic Theology*. Philadelphia: Fortress, 1975.

————. "The 'Literal Reading' of Biblical Narrative in the Christian Tradition: Does It Stretch or Will It Break?" In *The Bible and the Narrative Tradition*, edited by Frank McConnell, 36–77. Oxford: Oxford University Press, 1986.

Gadamer, Hans-Georg. *Truth and Method*. 2nd ed. Translated by William Glen-Doepel, edited by John Cumming and Garrett Barden. London: Sheed & Ward, 1979.

Grafton, Antony. *Defenders of the Text: The Traditions of Scholarship in an Age of Science*. Cambridge: Harvard University Press, 1991.

Graham, Nita. "Teaching against the Spirit of the Age: George Grant and the Museum Culture." In *George Grant and the Subversion of Modernity*, edited by Arthur Davis, 285–303. Toronto: University of Toronto Press, 1996.

Grant, George Parkin. "Faith and Multiversity." In *Technology and Justice*, 35–77. Notre Dame, IN: University of Notre Dame Press, 1986.

Gross, David L. *The Past in Ruins: Tradition and the Critique of Modernity*. Amherst: University of Massachusetts Press, 1992.

Gunton, Colin E. *A Brief Theology of Revelation*. Edinburgh: T&T Clark, 1995.

Gustafson, James M. *Intersections: Science, Theology, and Ethics*. Cleveland: Pilgrim, 1996.

Hauerwas, Stanley. "Positioning: In the Church and University, but Not of Either." In *Dispatches from the Front: Theological Engagements with the Secular*, 5–28. Durham, NC: Duke University Press, 1994.

Heelas, Paul, Scott Lash, and Paul Morris, eds. *Detraditionalization: Critical Reflections on Authority and Identity*. Oxford: Blackwell, 1996.

Heidegger, Martin. "Phenomenology and Theology." In *The Piety of Thinking: Essays by Martin Heidegger*, edited by James G. Hart and John C. Maraldo, 5–21. Bloomington: Indiana University Press, 1976.

Jeanrond, Werner. *Text and Interpretation as Categories of Theological Thinking*. Dublin: Gill & Macmillan, 1988.

———. *Theological Hermeneutics: Development and Significance*. London: SCM, 1994.

Jenson, Robert W. "The Church and the Sacraments." In *The Cambridge Companion to Christian Doctrine*, edited by Colin E. Gunton, 205–27. Cambridge: Cambridge University Press, 1997.

Johnson, Luke Timothy. "Imagining the World Scripture Imagines." *Modern Theology* 14 (1998): 165–80.

Jones, Serene. *Calvin and the Rhetoric of Piety*. Louisville: Westminster John Knox, 1995.

Jüngel, Eberhard. "The Dogmatic Significance of the Question of the Historical Jesus." In *Theological Essays II*, edited with an introduction by J. B. Webster, translated by J. B. Webster with Arnold Neufeld-Fast, 82–119. Edinburgh: T&T Clark, 1995.

———. "The Emergence of the New." In *Theological Essays II*, 35–58. Edinburgh: T&T Clark, 1995.

———. *Gott als Geheimnis der Welt: Zur Begründung der Theologie des Gekreuzigten im Streit zwischen Theismus und Atheismus*. Tübingen: Mohr Siebeck, 1977.

———. "Invocation of God as the Ethical Ground of Christian Action: Introductory Remarks on the Posthumous Fragments of Karl Barth's Ethics of the Doctrine of Reconciliation." In *Theological Essays I*, translated with an introduction by J. B. Webster, 154–72. Edinburgh: T&T Clark, 1989.

———. "The Revelation of the Hiddenness of God: A Contribution to the Protestant Understanding of the Hiddenness of Divine Action." In *Theological Essays II*, 120–44. Edinburgh: T&T Clark, 1995.

Kant, Immanuel. *The Conflict of the Faculties*. Translated and introduced by Mary J. Gregor. Lincoln: University of Nebraska Press, 1992.

———. *Critique of Pure Reason*. Translated by F. Max Müller. Garden City, NY: Doubleday, 1966.

———. *Religion within the Limits of Reason Alone*. New York: Harper & Row, 1960.

———. "What Is Enlightenment?" In *On History*, edited, introduced, and translated by Lewis White Beck, 3–10. New York: Macmillan, 1963.

Kelsey, David H. "The Bible and Christian Theology." *Journal of the American Academy of Religion* 48 (1980): 385–402.

————. "Church Discourse and Public Realm." In *Theology and Dialogue: Essays in Conversation with George Lindbeck*, edited by Bruce D. Marshall, 7–33. Notre Dame, IN: University of Notre Dame Press, 1990.

Kierkegaard, Søren. "Of the Difference between a Genius and an Apostle." In *The Present Age and Two Minor Ethico-Religious Treatises*, translated by Alexander Dru and Walter Lowrie, with an introduction by Charles Williams, 137–63. London: Oxford University Press, 1940.

————. *Training in Christianity, and the Edifying Discourse Which "Accompanied" It*. Translated by Walter Lowrie. Princeton: Princeton University Press, 1944.

Lash, Nicholas. "Performing the Scriptures." In *Theology on the Way to Emmaus*, 37–46. London: SCM, 1986.

Lindbeck, George. "Scripture, Consensus, and Community." In *Biblical Interpretation in Crisis: The Ratzinger Conference on Bible and Church*, edited by Richard John Neuhaus, 74–101. Grand Rapids: Eerdmans, 1989.

Lundin, Roger. *The Culture of Interpretation: Christian Faith and the Postmodern World*. Grand Rapids: Eerdmans, 1993.

Luther, Martin. *Three Treatises*. Translated by Charles M. Jacobs, A. T. W. Steinhäuser, and W. A. Lambert. Philadelphia: Fortress, 1970.

MacIntyre, Alasdair. *Three Rival Versions of Moral Enquiry: Encyclopaedia, Genealogy, and Tradition*. Notre Dame, IN: University of Notre Dame Press, 1990.

Manguel, Alberto. *A History of Reading*. London: HarperCollins, 1996.

Martin, Thomas F. "'An Abundant Supply of Discourse': Augustine and the Rhetoric of Monasticism." *Downside Review* 116, no. 402 (1998): 7–25.

Nagel, Thomas. *The View from Nowhere*. Oxford: Oxford University Press, 1986.

Nichols, Aidan. "T. S. Eliot and Yves Congar on the Nature of Tradition." In *Scribe of the Kingdom: Essays on Theology and Culture*, vol. 1, 78–89. London: Sheed & Ward, 1994.

Niebuhr, H. Richard. *Faith on Earth: An Inquiry into Faith on Earth*. Edited by Richard R. Niebuhr. New Haven: Yale University Press, 1989.

————. *The Meaning of Revelation*. New York: Macmillan, 1962.

————. *Radical Monotheism and Western Culture*. New York: Harper, 1960.

Nussbaum, Martha C. *Cultivating Humanity: A Classical Defense of Reform in Liberal Education*. Cambridge: Harvard University Press, 1997.

Oakeshott, Michael. *The Voice of Poetry in the Conversation of Mankind: An Essay*. London: Bowes & Bowes, 1959.

Pelikan, Jaroslav. *The Idea of the University: A Reexamination*. New Haven: Yale University Press, 1992.

————. *The Vindication of Tradition*. New Haven: Yale University Press, 1984.

Placher, William C. *The Domestication of Transcendence: How Modern Thinking about God Went Wrong*. Louisville: Westminster John Knox, 1996.

Ratzinger, Joseph. "Revelation and Tradition." In *Revelation and Tradition*, edited by Karl Rahner and Joseph Ratzinger, 25–49. London: Burns & Oates, 1966.

Ricoeur, Paul. "The Task of Hermeneutics." In *Hermeneutics and the Human Sciences: Essays on Language, Action, and Interpretation*, edited, translated, and introduced by John B. Thompson, 43–62. Cambridge: Cambridge University Press, 1981.

————. "Toward a Hermeneutic of the Idea of Revelation." In *Essays on Biblical Interpretation*, edited by Lewis S. Mudge, 73–118. Philadelphia: Fortress, 1980.

Rorty, Amélie Oksenberg. "Moral Imperialism vs. Moral Conflict: Conflicting Aims of Education." In *Can Virtue Be Taught?*, edited by Barbara Darling-Smith, 33–51. Notre Dame, IN: University of Notre Dame Press, 1993.

Rorty, Richard. "Introduction: Antirepresentationalism, Ethnocentrism, and Liberalism." In *Objectivity, Relativism, and Truth: Philosophical Papers*, vol. 1, 1–17. Cambridge: Cambridge University Press, 1991.

Sauter, Gerhard. *Eschatological Rationality: Theological Issues in Focus*. Grand Rapids: Baker, 1996.

Schleiermacher, Friedrich. *The Christian Faith*. Edited by H. R. Mackintosh and J. S. Stewart. Edinburgh: T&T Clark, 1928.

Schner, George. *Education for Ministry: Reform and Renewal in Theological Education*. Kansas City, MO: Sheed & Ward, 1993.

Schutz, Alfred. "On Multiple Realities." In *The Collected Papers of Alfred Schutz*, vol. 1: *The Problem of Social Reality*, edited and introduced by Maurice Natanson, with a preface by H. L. Van Breda, 207–59. The Hague: Nijhoff, 1962.

Skinner, Quentin. *Reason and Rhetoric in the Philosophy of Hobbes.* Cambridge: Cambridge University Press, 1996.

Smith, Huston. "Educating the Intellect: On Opening the Eye of the Heart." In *Can Virtue Be Taught?*, edited by Barbara Darling-Smith, 17–31. Notre Dame, IN: University of Notre Dame Press, 1993.

Smith, Jonathan Z. *Map Is Not Territory: Studies in the History of Religion.* Leiden: Brill, 1978.

———. "Sacred Persistence: Toward a Redescription of Canon." In *Imagining Religion: From Babylon to Jonestown*, 36–52. Chicago: University of Chicago Press, 1982.

Springsted, Eric O. "Rootedness: Culture and Value." In *Simone Weil's Philosophy of Culture: Readings toward a Divine Humanity*, edited by Richard H. Bell, 161–88. Cambridge: Cambridge University Press, 1993.

Tanner, Kathryn. *God and Creation in Christian Theology: Tyranny or Empowerment?* Oxford: Blackwell, 1988.

———. *The Politics of God: Christian Theologies and Social Justice.* Minneapolis: Fortress, 1992.

———. *Theories of Culture: A New Agenda for Theology.* Minneapolis: Fortress, 1997.

Taylor, Charles. "Overcoming Epistemology." In *Philosophical Arguments*, 1–19. Cambridge: Harvard University Press, 1995.

Thiemann, Ronald F. *Revelation and Theology: The Gospel as Narrated Promise.* Notre Dame, IN: University of Notre Dame Press, 1985.

Torrance, Thomas F. "Questioning in Christ." In *Theology in Reconstruction*, 117–27. London: SCM, 1965.

———. *Theological Science.* Oxford: Oxford University Press, 1969.

Tracy, David. *The Analogical Imagination: Christian Theology and the Culture of Pluralism.* London: SCM, 1981.

———. *Plurality and Ambiguity: Hermeneutics, Religion, Hope.* San Francisco: Harper & Row, 1987.

Watson, Francis. "The Scope of Hermeneutics." In *The Cambridge Companion to Christian Doctrine*, edited by Colin E. Gunton, 65–80. Cambridge: Cambridge University Press, 1997.

Weil, Simone. *The Need for Roots: Prelude to a Declaration of Duties towards Mankind*. Translated by Arthur F. Wills, with a preface by T. S. Eliot. London: Routledge & Kegan Paul, 1952.

Wightman, W. P. D. *Science in a Renaissance Society*. London: Hutchinson, 1972.

Wiles, Maurice. "The Uses of 'Holy Scripture.'" In *Explorations in Theology*, vol. 4, 73–82. London: SCM, 1979.

Williams, Rowan. "The Incarnation as the Basis of Dogma." In *The Religion of the Incarnation: Anglican Essays in Commemoration of Lux Mundi*, edited by Robert Morgan, 85–98. Bristol: Bristol Classical Press, 1989.

Wolterstorff, Nicholas. *John Locke and the Ethics of Belief*. Cambridge: Cambridge University Press, 1996.

———. "The Travail of Theology in the Modern Academy." In *The Future of Theology: Essays in Honour of Jürgen Moltmann*, edited by Miroslav Volf, Carmen Krieg, and Thomas Kucharz, 35–46. Grand Rapids: Eerdmans, 1996.

Wood, Charles M. *The Formation of Christian Understanding: An Essay in Theological Hermeneutics*. Philadelphia: Westminster, 1981.

———. *Vision and Discernment: An Orientation in Theological Study*. Atlanta: Scholars Press, 1985.

Young, Frances. *The Art of Performance: Towards a Theology of Holy Scripture*. London: Darton, Longman & Todd, 1990.

Subject Index

Author Index